ALIGNING CULTURE & STRATEGY

How clarity, empathy and leadership drive high-performance

by Daniel Murray

empathic
CONSULTING

Contents

About this book   1

Part 1:

The Foundations of Culture   4

Chapter 1: Who is eating whom?   5

Rick's Rocky Road at Presta Materials   9

Chapter 2: The Aligned Organisation Model   13

Presta's Great Wall Of Values   17

Part 2:

The Meaning of Guiding Principles   22

Chapter 3: Bringing the words to life   23

Presta's New Guiding Principles   29

Chapter 4: Rivers Follow Riverbeds   32

Presta and Paying Attention To The Pain   36

Part 3:

Embedding Guiding Principles in Culture   40

Chapter 5: Realigning The Culture Flow   41

Adjusting Presta's Sails   44

Part 4:

Clarity, Empathy & Leadership   52

Chapter 6: Purposeful Performance   53

Part 5:

Managing the Inevitable Tension   74

Chapter 7: Stop Trying To Get People On Your Bus   75

Bumps In The Road   81

Part 6:

The Playbook   90

Chapter 8: Designing the framework for your culture 91

The Presta Playbook   107

So what next?   114

Presta Guiding Principles Playbook sample   116

About Empathic Consulting   132

About this book

Humans are amazing creatures. We're a remarkable success story. As individuals, humans are relatively slow, weak and unimpressive in all of their physical attributes when compared with much of the animal kingdom. However, in groups we are incredible! This strange mammal with the big brain has taken over the entire world.

It might be easy to put it all down to our brains, but actually it's our ability to work together that is the real magic of humans. Small groups of humans deeply connected through bloodlines, traditions, and shared rituals were able to overcome the most dramatic challenges, and help us build the complex modern world we live in today.

For modern organisations, the ability to bring a diverse group of people together to solve complex problems is critical to success, but many are struggling, rife with political in-fighting, disengaged employees, blown-out budgets, and projects that seem like they will never be delivered. How did our ancestors deal with challenges when we can't seem to get six people in a room together to decide on a name for our new website portal?

This book walks you through the experiences and methodologies we've created at Empathic Consulting to help organisations build strategies and cultures that can overcome those challenges and that embedded 'this is just the way we do things here' behaviour which slowly sucks down dynamic initiatives, projects and people – corporate quicksand.

Using a fictional narrative based on our experiences with clients, we walk you through the way Rick Hampton transformed his dysfunctional leadership team at the fictional company Presta Materials.

Our focus is on the leadership team. In many organisations, different divisions must coordinate closely to create desired outcomes. While processes and systems are critical, the ability to work together effectively comes down to the leaders of each area working together effectively to support their teams toward a shared outcome. If they can't, or won't, silos develop, followed not long after by a type of siege mentality.

Leadership teams are the heart of organisations, so our attention is concentrated on not only what individual leaders should focus on, but also how they should view the changes required in the broader leadership team to achieve long-term success.

Leaders and their leadership teams set the foundations for building an aligned organisation that drives sustained and purposeful performance. If you're wondering why your leadership team isn't performing as you believe it should, or you feel that something isn't quite right but are not sure what 'it' is, Aligning Culture and Strategy is a practical guide that will help you create more alignment in your leadership team and a better performing organisation.

This book presents the Aligned Organisation Model we have developed, and breaks down the two key elements of this model – the Tangible and Intangible – across the three phases: Planning, Execution and Outcome. I also include examples of organisations that have got this right, and others that have suffered the painful experience of divergence.

Highlights at the beginning of each section will help you find what you are looking for, and there is a set of questions and actions at the end of each section to encourage you to act promptly to improve the alignment of your organisation.

As John Maxwell so elegantly put it: "Pessimists will complain about the wind. Optimists will hope it will change. Leaders will adjust the sails." This book will help you recognise which ropes to pull to adjust your sails and lead your team through the storms ahead.

For more information go to our website:
www.empathicconsulting.com

Daniel Murray

Part 1
The Foundations of Culture

Chapter 1

Who is eating whom?

Highlights

- Culture is a powerful element in any successful organisation
- Changing that culture takes more than an internal marketing campaign
- Building alignment is the critical factor for success.

"If you see your company culture as a family, you don't want to fire someone just because their short-term performance is not good. If you do, even the people on your team who are excellent performers will look at what's going on and say, 'Someday you might fire me too.' You'll lose everyone's trust."

Eric Yuan, CEO of Zoom

No doubt, if you have flicked through popular business books or LinkedIn posts, you have come across this quote from legendary management consultant, Peter Drucker:

"Culture eats strategy for breakfast."

This plea for organisations to take culture seriously has encouraged many frustrated people leaders and HR teams around the world to demand more attention, budget, and leadership commitment in order to build a positive work culture.

However, building culture is hard and often simply ends up with brand new inspirational posters on walls, token gestures in tea rooms and some new furniture. Sadly, the excitement of mountaintop photos with someone arms akimbo looking towards an amazing sunrise, bean bags and ping pong tables is short-lived. All too often, vibrant hopes of lasting change are dashed by embedded sets of rigid policies, persistent KPIs and powerful hierarchical structures that have long reigned supreme in many organisations, old and not so old.

Despite the culture-focused efforts of passionate followers of Drucker, the relentless drumbeat of systems, processes and procedures wear down the teeth of this new culture as it tries to consume the strategy - Mr Drucker's cultural movement can swiftly become the victim. People who are accustomed to 'the way we've always done things around here' may quickly dismiss the new culture drive as nothing more than another HR fad, a waste of money, and a distraction from "real work". People soon forget the posters and call people playing ping pong lazy – worse still, they actively sabotage such efforts in the knowledge that if they just hang in there long enough, and don't engage at all or undermine the process, they'll live through another cultural change initiative. The result? The bright light of promise fades, and cultural change disappears with a final plop under the quicksand.

But don't think that means culture isn't a powerful force that can drive performance. The issue is not whether strategy or culture should prevail in some fictitious battle royale - we shouldn't be choosing between one or the other, and successful organisations do not build one at the cost of the other. Successful organisations know that a powerful strategy needs to be supported by a powerful and aligned culture.

The main issue we have had the opportunity to help change in a number of organisations is that their strategy and culture were designed independently and have become misaligned - if they were ever truly aligned in the first place. The wonderful culture designed in a workshop may not fit in with

Aligning Culture & Strategy

the existing structures and strategies of the organisation, but changing one requires a change in the other, and trying to change one while ignoring the other is a recipe for lacklustre performance, and a decline in responsiveness to customers when there are changes in the competitive environment, technology and innovation.

If you want a culture of collaboration, but focus incentives and rewards on individual effort, you have misalignment. If you want a culture of incredible customer service but set targets for the length of time people are on the phone, you will develop misalignment. If you ask people to be innovative, but constrain ideas with layers of committees and bureaucracy, you have misalignment. Misalignment breeds dissonance leading to disengagement and erosion of performance.

On the flip side, when an organisation is able to build a high-performance culture that supports their strategies, they are unstoppable. Take Zoom for example, a company that clearly benefited from the Covid-19 pandemic. You can see how growing from ten million users a day to over 200 million in a month would be great for the bottom line, but also create an incredible strain on your team.

Consider the number of customer service calls increasing by more than twenty times overnight, and processing transactions, account changes, security risks, and complaints all growing exponentially. Despite this, Zoom has an employee net promoter (eNPS) score of 90! In contrast, a competitor, Webex, who were also riding the wave of the pandemic slumped to an eNPS of -34.

Zoom have focused on maintaining their culture during this period of unprecedented growth. They continue to offer flexibility and employee benefits despite the incredible growth. Leaders across the organisation remain focused on caring for their customers, and Zoom were awarded the Best Company Leadership Award in addition to the Best Place to Work Award 2021.

Zoom do not trade off their culture for performance; they ensure their culture is a key driver of their performance. They have built systems and processes that fit their culture and reinforce the values of the organisation, and while many companies complain that Zoom meetings are killing their culture, the company itself uses its own platforms to enhance engagement. Their Happiness Crew, a group of company volunteers, sets up fun and engaging activities on Zoom, because the Zoom team doesn't dwell on challenges, it looks for solutions through the lens of Zoom's core value: care.

Whether you are running a start-up or managing an existing organisation, leading at at time of incredible growth or looking for the next opportunity, building alignment between your strategy and culture is paramount. Let's see how we guided our fictional general manager, Rick Hampton of Presta Materials, to manage misalignment in his organisation.

Aligning Culture & Strategy

Rick's Rocky Road at Presta Materials

I walked into the busy café and scanned the room, looking for my old friend, Rick Hampton. Rick and I had played football together a few years back, and he had recently been promoted to the position of general manager for a medium-sized manufacturing company, Presta Materials.

Rick had been at Presta Materials for the last decade, working his way up from a position in sales to taking over the management of the company after the previous managing director had retired. Presta manufactured materials for the building and construction industry, distributing their products through a large network of dealers across three countries.

When I sat down at the table, I saw a weight of concern that I didn't remember from our sporting days on my old friend's face . He looked tired and stressed, and his fingers tapped a rhythm on the table like a heavy metal drummer mid-set. When he looked up to greet me, the worry in his eyes was apparent.

"Hey, how's the new job going?" I asked, skipping the small talk as I suspected he wasn't looking for a social catch-up.

"Yeah, that's why I called. I know you don't usually work with manufacturing businesses, but I was wondering if I could pick your brain for some ideas?" pleaded Rick.

While it is true that I had mainly worked with financial services companies, the reality is that leading and maintaining a culture that drives performance involves a set of steps and skills applicable in almost any industry.

"Rick, I help leaders, in particular their leadership teams, to develop a culture and strategy that will drive performance," I replied with a smile to ease his nervous energy. "Culture is a phenomenon that exists whenever you bring a group of people together, so as long as you have people in your organisation, I'm pretty sure that I can help. What's going on?"

"I feel like things are all over the place. My sales team is frustrated with the operations team, and our manufacturing plant can't get raw materials from suppliers to keep production levels up. I'm getting calls from our distributors asking when their orders will arrive, and, honestly, I have no idea what to tell them. It's like in the last month we've gone from boom to bust, and I can't stop it." Rick paused. I think he realised he had, for the first time in a long time, been able to actually talk about all the problems that were constantly spinning in his mind.

"You've got a lot going on. It must be hard to manage. How's the family?" I could see the toll on Rick.

"They are my rock as usual, but I do worry about what will happen if the stress can't be reduced." I could see emotion building in Rick's face.

"Let's have a chat and see if I can help. First we need to understand what's not working in your team. It sounds like there are a lot of external pressures that we could blame, but the reality I see for most of my clients is that, for starters..." I drew a large circle on the notepad I'd pulled out while I was talking. "This is the external environment around your organisation and, for you and almost everyone else in the world today, it's a chaotic and volatile mess that you can never really control. But what you can have some control over is this much smaller environment," and I drew a smaller circle within the larger one.

"That feels just as chaotic as the big one!" Rick smiled, the humour relaxing him slightly.

"It may well be now, and without strong and cohesive leadership it will probably become more chaotic as the influence of the outside world pushes in on it. Our job is not to look out into the chaos to ask it to stop," I said, drawing little arrows from the edge of the small circle out into the larger one. "It's to focus on building a stronger team here, where we can have greater influence and control." I highlighted my point by shading the small circle.

I turned over to a new page, and said:

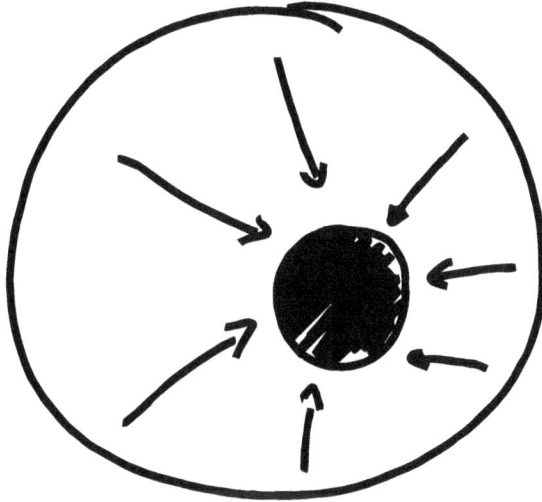

"Let's start to unpack what may be causing the chaos in this inner circle, and how we can bring back a bit more order."

Rick leaned forward in his chair, a glimmer of hope in his smile, but only a glimmer. We had a lot of work to do.

Are you feeling overwhelmed by all the changes in your organisation?

- Focus on what you can control; you can't change the whole world

- External pressures put a greater strain on organisations, and will expose weaknesses in your team cohesion

- A strong leadership team is vital to coordinating and actioning an organisational response.

Chapter 2

The Aligned Organisation Model

———

Highlights

- Organisations move through three phases: from planning to execution to outcomes

- Even a great strategy and a brilliant culture may only work if they are in alignment

- We must examine how our values and culture support or diverge from our strategy and operating model.

"Determine what behaviors and beliefs you value as a company, and have everyone live true to them. These behaviors and beliefs should be so essential to your core, that you don't even think of it as culture."

Brittany Forsyth, VP of Human Relations, Shopify

No matter the industry, when you bring a large group of people together in one organisation to achieve a common goal, you create a hugely complex situation very quickly. There are individuals working in teams, and teams forming divisions. People are busy running processes and systems, solving problems, and responding to work from other teams. This is a large messy group of people, often frantically busy, but, if it all goes well, there is a successful outcome.

While this complexity is real, and we dare not underplay the variety it creates for almost all organisations, there are three very simple, high-level phases we watch them progress through.

- Planning: Where we decide how we will play in the market, what our strategy will be and what values and vision underpin our sense of purpose

- Execution: Where the rubber hits the road, our plans become reality, and our culture and operations become action

- Outcomes: This is where we see the fruit of our labours, and can measure our performance and sense of purpose.

So often though, we forget that each of these three phases has two dimensions: the Tangible and the Intangible. The Tangible Dimension is built, measured and maintained with structure and rules. This is where we develop strategic goals, targets, rules, policies and processes.

The strategy of an organisation is developed in the planning phase, and then an operating model, consisting of the processes, systems, hierarchies and plans, is required to deliver this strategy. If the operating model delivers the strategy successfully, it should lead to a measurable, tangible performance.

The Intangible Dimension consists of the powerful elements that we can't measure easily. Our values, relationships, culture, and sense of purpose are all vital to long-term success, but challenging to measure with any accuracy.

As with the strategy, the values of the organisation are developed in the planning phase, and then, through people's actions and behaviours aligning to these values, an organisation creates its own culture - the way things are done. If this culture is aligned with their values, they will deliver on their organisational purpose, and their outcomes will be true to their values.

The diagram below is the Aligned Organisation Model that shows these Tangible and Intangible elements across the three phases of Planning, Execution and Outcomes. It also highlights the main challenge we see in so many organisations: the red arrows diverging in the execution phase represent the lack of alignment between the culture we desire and the operating model we have developed. This misalignment usually occurs in the execution, and not the planning phase. We consistently observe that it occurs when, during the complexity that execution presents, the actions and behaviours that correspond to the operating model do not align with the values of the organisation, so that the culture is misaligned.

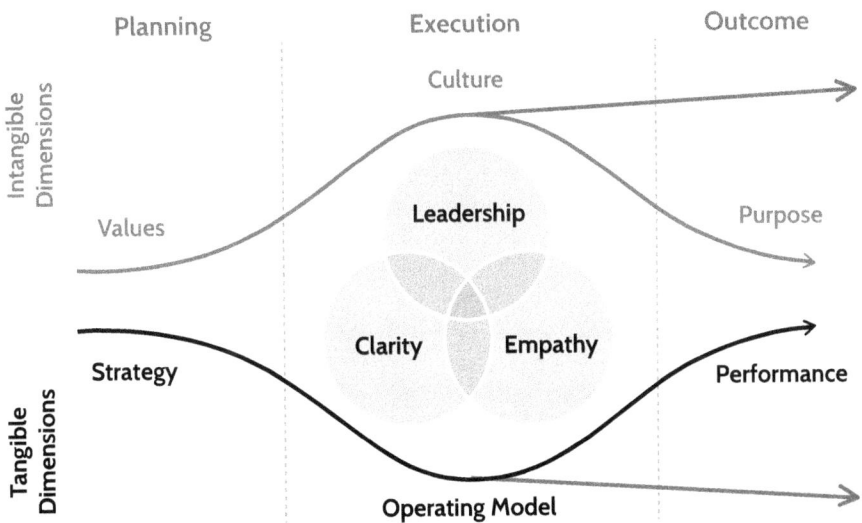

In the centre, we have highlighted three key drivers every organisation should foster to support alignment and congruence through execution and into the outcome phase.

An Aligned Organisation ensures your culture and strategy are working together to drive both purpose and performance. They should reinforce each other, and when they start to diverge leaders need to realise, and identify the issues, and have the skills to correct them. A sense of congruence is there when things are as they should be, supporting sustained and purposeful performance in an aligned organisation.

Does your organisation feel like that? If not, keep reading.

Presta's Great Wall Of Values

I went to see Rick at his office a week later to continue exploring ways we could work together to bring some clarity to the chaos in his team. The first thing that struck me was the massive wall of words behind the reception desk. It was a colourful collection of positive sounding words that you might expect to see on affirmation cards.

In bright orange was the word 'Positive'. Next to it, 'Teamwork' in deep blue, and 'Customers' in lime green. 'Results' was next in red, and so they continued. In all, I counted about two dozen colourful words on that wall. At the very top 'Our Values' were in bold black.

"That's quite a wall of words," I said to Rick, pointing to the noisy word soup behind him.

"Yeah, we asked each person in the company to tell us what they thought our values were. It's been up there for a few years now. We may need to redo it at some stage." Rick seemed a little dismissive of the wall of values as he picked up his notebook and we headed to the boardroom.

"How do you remember what they all are?" I asked as we went in and closed the door.

"Remember what?" Rick asked, clearly focused on other issues.

"The values. How does anyone remember what the values are when there are so many of them?" I was pushing, wanting to understand more about these colourful words.

"I don't think anyone does, to be honest. It was a fun exercise when we did it, but now that everyone is so busy, I think we just focus on getting the work done," Rick continued, sitting down at the large wooden desk and pouring us each a glass of water.

"Why did you put them up? What were you hoping to achieve?" I went on pushing for an explanation, but could see that Rick wasn't as interested in the values as I was.

"I don't really know. I think someone thought it would be a good way to get everybody to contribute to something. Don't you think company values are important?" Rick replied, my questions about the wall clearly frustrating him.

"They are very important," I replied, "but not as a cluster of words on the wall that no one can remember. To be useful, everyone must know them, understand them, and use them as a guide to respond, behave and make decisions in their daily work. It's not the quantity nor even the quality of the words that matter. It's whether people can turn them into actions, and how these actions shape the culture you are looking to build. If you have a lot of nice words that can be flexed to cover just about any action, you don't have a set of values, you just have a word soup. If your salespeople are torn about whether to offer a discount to an old client or not, which word on the wall helps them make the decision? Do they give the discount and say they were focusing on 'Customer', or not give it and say they were focusing on 'Results'?"

"Right. I hadn't really thought about it that way," Rick replied.

"So, which one would you want them to choose? Results or Customer?" I went on pushing to make my point.

"Well, it depends. They would probably just come to me, and I'd make a call," Rick replied, now leaning into this conversation on values.

"Okay, which values would you use to make a decision? What would you say?" I was still pushing Rick to think about the situation.

"It actually happens all the time at the moment, and it's a really complex question. Our relationships with so many of our different customers are in

Aligning Culture & Strategy

a bit of a mess, and I'd need to check things like the volume we currently have with them, their growth potential, and how loyal they've been to us over the years." Rick leant back in his chair, seeming pleased to be sharing a snapshot of the level of complexity he was facing in everyday operations with me.

"Rick, if all of these decisions need to come to you, and the complexity is so great, how will you ever be able to get on top of things, let alone grow? If your people can only follow set rules, and can't make decisions in ambiguous situations, then they're just cogs in a big machine. If you're making all the decisions at the centre, you're going to hold this machine back. No wonder you're feeling stressed. You're trying to run this whole business by yourself. I know you're a talented guy, but this might be an area we should look to change first. You don't need a wall of values, you need a set of guiding principles," I said this soothingly, knowing that it might put Rick on the back foot, but fortunately he could see the problem I was describing clearly, and it was as though a weight had been lifted from his shoulders.

"How will guiding principles be able to help though?" Rick seemed puzzled. "Don't we need a set of policies or processes to manage these decisions? Shouldn't we take the decisions out of the hands of individuals so we get a level of consistency?"

"You can, and maybe you should. The first thing I would ask is, can you? Could we possibly sit down and write a set of rules that would cover all the decisions you need to make in this complex business?" I reopened my notebook at the page with the two circles, and pointed at the inner circle. "Remember how complex and chaotic this small circle is today? And even if we did that, remember that the outside world keeps changing too. The rate of change in this external environment is faster than ever before. I can see you spending a lot of time and effort codifying all the rules in this inner circle, only for the outer circle to change so much that you'd need to start all over again. Do you think that could happen?"

"Actually, that's exactly what has happened," Rick said. "We used to have a pretty clear set of pricing rules, but new products, aggressive competitors, and demanding customers have seen that bent out of shape. We basically don't even look at it anymore." He laughed, seeing the reality of the challenge.

"The good news is, that happens in most companies. The bad news is, few of them know what to do about it," I replied.

"But you know, don't you?" Rick asked, almost sarcastically.

"Well, to put it simply, no. No one can really create a perfect business with rules and policies alone, because of the incredibly complex systems at play that are constantly adapting. Rules and policies are vital - they create structure and rigidity, which are useful in certain places and conditions, but we live in a VUCA world. VUCA stands for volatile, uncertain, complex and ambiguous. During my undergraduate degree, I studied Chaos Theory. It's an interesting, if pretty nerdy, area of mathematics that is actually pretty useful in a modern VUCA world. What you learn about systems like this is that you can't control them, but you can try to understand them. Organisations can't control the outside world, and you can only influence and predict certain parts of the system over small segments of time. When the environment is highly complex and chaotic, we need to make sure that our internal environment is adaptive and predictable. This is where guiding principles beat policies and rules all day long." I could see that Rick was somewhere between intrigued and confused.

"So, what are the right guiding principles for us?" Rick asked, probably bored I was talking about mathematics, and keen to get some answers.

"It depends. We need a set of guiding principles that align with your strategy," I said as I wrote a simple equation in my notebook:

$$GP + S = A$$

"When you have guiding principles that support your strategy, you get alignment. Your guiding principles are not just a list of words: the most effective guiding principles tend to short phrases that help you and everyone else in the organisation to navigate through a VUCA world in a consistent way, the Presta way. To start with, explain more about what's going on today, and what you want for the future." I urged Rick to sit down again, and started to talk about current challenges.

The Big Question & Actions

Do your values help your people to do the right thing, or are they a set of nice words on the wall?

- Ask your people if they know the values, what they mean and how they use them regularly

- If people always have to come to you for decisions, you need to build guiding principles that support decisions

- Build guiding principles that help people take action and make decisions when faced with complex situations.

Part 2

The Meaning of
Guiding Principles

Chapter 3

Bringing the words to life

Highlights

- While most organisations have a set of company values, few use them effectively
- When values are ineffective, good people can do terrible things by focusing on generating outcomes
- There are three key questions that ensure your guiding principles can be effectively used to shape your culture.

"We believe that it's really important to come up with core values that you can commit to. And by commit, we mean that you're willing to hire and fire based on them. If you're willing to do that, then you're well on your way to building a company culture that is in line with the brand you want to build."

Tony Hsieh, CEO, Zappos

Integrity - Service - Courage - Achievement - One Team
Integrity - Collaboration - Accountability - Respect - Excellence
Integrity - Collaboration - Excellence - Accountability - Service

The above words are the values of three different Australian companies. These three companies are all very large and successful businesses, dominating their industries. You may think that these values are all very similar. Maybe they are similar to your organisation's values too? I shouldn't be surprised. These words are common choices for many organisations.

You may also think that these all look like good values, good words, fine words. I don't think there is anything particularly wrong with them as words, however, words alone are not enough.

The three companies with these values are Westpac, ANZ, and the Commonwealth Bank of Australia. These were the values on their website, on the posters on their walls, and in their investor briefings before, during and after the Royal Commission into Banking.

The Royal Commission was a devastating set of revelations for the banks, showing that while these words were prominent on walls, websites and presentations, they were not lived in decision-making processes throughout their organisations. Let's look at just a few disconnects between the values and actions of the banks:

Offering a debt-ridden customer who had maxed out his credit card and admitted he was a problem gambler a $35,000 limit increase. Is this respect?

Selling insurance products to vulnerable customers who, within their own product conditions, were explicitly excluded from ever being able to make a claim on this insurance product. Is that integrity?

How about charging a customer who had died for financial advice? Is that service? It sounds like going way over and above, don't you think?

The fines and remediation paid by the banks due to the findings of the Banking Royal Commission cost their shareholders hundreds of millions of dollars. I'm sure that is not the type of accountability they had imagined when developing the values.

Values are so often a collection of nice words that few people challenge, but, much like their counterpart in the planning phase, strategy, they don't mean a thing until they are tested in the day-to-day interactions between company representatives, customers, colleagues, regulators, the community. They only come to life if they form the backbone of your culture.

Here are a few simple questions to ask about your values today:

- Can everyone remember them?
- Does everyone know what they actually mean?
- Do they clearly encourage certain behaviours?
- Does everyone use them to guide their behaviours?

If any of these are not answered with a strong yes, you've got work to do on redeveloping your values into guiding principles. When organisations ask me to help them refresh their values, I am always cautious. Sometimes this means they want me to come in, run a survey with all the staff to build a new long list of words, and reduce them with a thesaurus to just combine words and look for something 'fresh'.

I'm then asked to present these selected words to the Leadership Team, who debate the importance of the tense or pluralisation of each word, and compare them with the words of their most admired competitors, and there are the refreshed values.

I decline such assignments as this approach won't help. It's not effective, and shows a lack of genuine leadership and commitment. Changing the words on the walls from one set that no one remembers or uses to make decisions to a new set that are ignored too is a pointless exercise - good for my consulting fees, but terrible for the organisation.

Instead, I ask potential clients questions about the values or guiding principles they currently have:

Q1- Is this really a choice?

Strategy guru Michael Porter says "strategy is all about making choices, trade-offs; it's about deliberately choosing to be different." It is vital in choosing a strategy to determine not only what you are choosing to do, but what you are therefore choosing not to do.

I believe guiding principles should have a similar set of properties when we develop them. So often, an organisation's guiding principles are less of a choice, and more of a simple expectation.

Let's take integrity, for example. Is this really a choice? Don't all your customers and suppliers expect you to have integrity? If your competitors chose to describe their values as deceitful, then maybe you would have a case, but choosing integrity is much like choosing a value of law abiding... it's not a value; it's an expectation.

Making sure guiding principles are choices is important, because they need to be actively used. They are the guidelines that help your people make decisions.

You can choose to be fast and messy or slow and meticulous. You can be Customer First or Employee First. You can be Risk Takers or Risk Adverse. There are many choices, and none are wrong, but they all clarify what type of organisation you are going to be.

Q2 - Do they provide clarity?

The second question on your values is about clarity. Do your people understand what your values mean and how to use them? Guiding principles reduce ambiguity.

Many years ago, I was working for an organisation that had 'Brave' as one of its newly minted values. Brave sounds good, and most of us would like to be brave or think we are.

One day in a meeting, someone was obnoxious to a colleague, belittling their point of view in front of the entire team. When that person was called out for poor behaviour, their response was "I was just being brave!"

Aligning Culture & Strategy

As you may guess, this wasn't the intention of the value, but you can also see that without greater clarity a single word is always open to interpretation. You may also imagine that a value like Respect would be interpreted as being professional and courteous to your peers. But Respect can also mean never challenging people in positions of authority. You might want one and not the other, but your single word value doesn't provide the necessary clarity.

Clarity requires more content and context, in this way guiding principles are more useful than values. Describing your guiding principles in stories and specific situations is useful, and in my experience guiding principles fixed through real-life stories work best. Some organisations, such as Zappos. com, collate stories that define their guiding principles and culture. They are compiled into a beautiful book given to all employees every year.

One of our clients has a set of stories they tell every new employee to help bring clarity to the 'way we do things around here'. Reinforcing guiding principles with stories taps into the primal parts of our brain that are receptive to this ancient art, but however you provide it, clarity is vital.

Q3 - Are they seen in action?

My favourite example of guiding principles in action was a story in Tony Hsieh of Zappo's book *Delivering Happiness*. After a conference, Tony and a few other out-of-towners were in a hotel, and they all wanted pizza, but no one knew any pizzerias that would deliver in the area. Tony suggested one of them call his team at Zappos.

While renowned for selling shoes, Zappos didn't do pizza delivery, and the hungry conference-goers thought Tony was crazy, but he insisted they try. After an initial moment of confusion, the Zappos team member asked the caller to hold. While the room listened in on the speakerphone, he came back after a few seconds and said: "Do you have a pen? Here are three places near you still delivering pizza. Have a great night and thanks for your call."

There is no policy for what to do when someone calls for a pizza. There is no KPI or bonus system for helping strange callers. The Zappos employee was just living the core principle of the organisation: To live and deliver WOW.

Your written values may be the most elegantly designed and beautifully crafted in the world, but if they do not become clear commitments and consistent behaviours they are not your lived guiding principles, and they will not be representative of your culture.

The critical difference between intended values and lived culture is action. If the values become clear commitments, this shapes them into guiding principles people can use. This encourages more consistent behaviours, it is these behaviours that will shape your culture. If they don't shape action, they are probably just expensive posters and visuals.

Leaders play a critical role in implanting guiding principles into team culture by communicating constantly to ensure there is clarity on what the guiding principles are, what they mean, and how to translate them into shared commitments and behaviours relevant to that specific team. It is not enough to have vague ideas; leaders need to discuss and demonstrate what each principle means in the team context. "Delivering WOW" in the accounting team may look very different to the marketing team, and it's a leader's job to set expectations and commitments.

Leaders are also accountable for monitoring the behaviours of their people, and providing feedback on the alignment of behaviour with these guiding principles. If your people are living the guiding principles, a leader must provide recognition and praise, highlighting this to the rest of the team. If your people are acting out behaviours that are not aligned with the guiding principles, and especially if they are in conflict with them, it is the leader's job to give feedback, and demand alignment of behaviours to the guiding principles.

Guiding principles may be written by the Executive Team and rolled out on posters, but they are only embedded into culture through the constant efforts of people leaders, who persistently clarify, monitor and manage the behaviours of their people.

Aligning Culture & Strategy

Presta's New guiding principles

It was a Thursday afternoon in the Presta boardroom, and I was standing at the whiteboard with a blue marker while Rick talked about a number of challenging situations they had been through over the last few months. I wrote down some keywords, and questioned him on each scenario.

"Okay, what should they have done?" I asked repeatedly, sometimes to Rick's frustration as for him it seemed so obvious.

In one specific scenario, Rick described how a member of his team had damaged a glass door when delivering goods to a client.

"It wasn't even our customer's door. As he was leaving, the trolley he was pushing cracked a small glass panel on their neighbour's storefront. It wasn't a big piece of glass, but it was clearly broken. He just took off and hoped no one would notice," Rick said getting a little worked up.

"Okay, what should he have done?" I asked again.

Rick looked at me like I was joking. "He should have owned up straight away, given them his details, and reported it when he came back to the office so we could fix it. We always put things right here." Rick finished his sentence by pointing at the desk with his index finger.

"I think we might have your first value," I said to Rick with a smile.

"We always put things right?" Rick suddenly realised the gravitas of his words.

"Yes. That's a powerful value that will work as a guiding principle, don't you think? So everyone in the company knows that, while we make mistakes from time to time, we are always committed to putting things right. Whether it be an accident, a pricing error or an unhappy customer experience, we put things right. This guides people towards a common path. This is what a good guiding principle does," I said as Rick's face lighted up.

"Yeah, I really like that. I can see it as a tagline that our clients would appreciate." Rick nodded. "But don't we need everyone to vote on it? I don't want to impose anything on them. That's why we asked them for values last time."

"Let me ask two questions. Firstly, do you ask everyone to vote on your strategy, pricing or budgets?" I asked, knowing the answer was no. "Secondly, after you asked everyone to contribute and vote last time, did it actually change people's behaviour? For some reason, companies are hierarchical about strategy, and then want to become democratic about guiding principles, and that rarely ends well."

We continued to explore different scenarios, and decisions that Rick thought people should make consistently. It was a messy discussion, and contentious. After about two hours, I could tell Rick was running out of steam. We had developed around ten potential guiding principles, and he was wondering what was coming next.

"Let's put things on hold for today," I suggested. "I'll type these up and send them to you tonight. I recommend you sleep on the list, and reflect on it over the weekend. Let's have a call on Monday to chat through any thoughts and feedback, and then set up a meeting with your leadership team next Thursday."

"Right," responded Rick, "I'm keen to know what that meeting looks like though as they can be a tough group." Rick was concerned that his leadership team might be hard to manage in a discussion like this. It wasn't how they had operated previously, and they wouldn't be expecting it.

"Don't worry, Rick, it won't be a long discussion like this one. This next meeting will be more about listening to the challenges they see in the team today, bringing them up to speed with the changes you think we need to make, and highlighting the importance of their actions as a leadership team to embed real change. I've run a number of sessions like this, and I'm confident I can make the discussion productive," I said reassuringly.

As Rick walked with me out, I asked one more question.

"Rick, do you think any of your leadership team are going to really resist this sort of change?"

"Good question. While we were talking, I thought of one of them in particular - Jim Popovski, our Head of Operations, has been visibly frustrated in meetings lately. He may be a little annoyed that we're talking about guiding principles when there are so many issues in the supply chain." Rick seemed to feel the weight of the issues fall back on his shoulders as he spoke.

"Great to know. Maybe I can grab a coffee with him next week before the session. Can you introduce us? Send us both an email, and I'll call him tomorrow," I said to Rick as we shook hands and I headed back to my car.

The Big Question & Actions

Do you need to work with your leadership team on a set of guiding principles for your organisation?

- Look for examples of actions and behaviours that are not aligned with your expectations

- Consider principles that would give your people a better understanding of appropriate actions

- Avoid developing your guiding principles through simply asking everyone what they want.

Chapter 4

Rivers Follow Riverbeds

"When values, thoughts, feelings, and actions are in alignment, a person becomes focused and character is strengthened."

John C. Maxwell

Culture is a powerful force. As social creatures, humans take cues from those around them on what to do, and we readily develop and follow group norms. When these norms are based on specific sets of shared guiding principles and beliefs, culture can be a massive driver of purposeful performance.

However, culture is always evolving, moving and changing. Culture is defined by what people do, how they do it, and how others feel about these actions. Your culture is defined by the next million little things that happen, and everything counts - every conversation, meeting, email, decision, greeting in the hallway. Everything that happens around us influences us in sometimes subtle and subconscious ways, but they all matter.

Unlike policies and procedures, you can't set and forget when it comes to culture. You constantly need to be aware of it, monitor it and influence it. But the influences that drive culture are not the only intangible factors - your strategic decisions and operating model choices have an impact too.

In many ways, the relationship between culture and the operating model is akin to a river. Culture is the water, fast-moving, dynamic and strong - always changing, ebbing and flowing over time, but one thing about rivers is that they follow riverbeds.

Your operating model is like the riverbed. It is the structure that underpins the way you and your people operate. I've worked with groups of wonderful people who, with the best of intentions, built a set of values that are beautiful and inspiring, however they failed to adjust the processes, systems and standards of the past, and suffer the lasting consequences of misalignment.

Let me give you a prime example from the world of sales: this team was a great bunch of people who cared about each other and their clients. When I worked with them, we explored the activities and processes that really influenced them. We were looking for the big items that they thought about often, and the things that kept them awake at night. Their list is probably not surprising, and focus areas and activities featured were:

- Sales Targets - which linked their personal performance to their monthly commission payment

- Sales Meetings - which mainly involved the general manager asking each team member how they were doing on targets

- Prospecting - where each of the sales people scoured databases for potential clients so they could flag them and block the others from contacting them.

That was not all they did in the working week, but they said these were major factors that influenced their activities and focus, and really shaped what they did, and how they felt about their performance.

I asked the team to describe how they experienced these elements of their operating model, and the results were unsurprising: they described sales targets and commissions as an individualistic way to compare, and to compete against each other, and said sales meetings were regular and very public reminders of how they were tracking against their peers.

Interestingly, prospecting was seen purely as each salesperson looking after their own patch, and tagging potential clients in the shared customer management system so that the rest of the team couldn't proactively approach them. On reflection, the team described it as self-serving protectionism.

Although each of these very influential and commonly experienced elements of their operating model reinforced feelings of competition, individualism and self-protection, the team's values were: Collaboration and Teamwork, Customer Centricity, Passionate about People, and Celebrate Success. It was immediately clear to everyone in the room when we wrote these down that they might be aware of, and even truly desire, their values, but they were not actively living nor experiencing them.

This is obviously not unusual. Many organisations have posters that highlight integrity and honesty, while they maintain policies and processes that don't enforce accountability, and restrict the flow of information throughout the organisation. Others have call centre walls covered with the words 'Customer First', but the glaring lights of the contact centre dashboard beam live data as to how many calls each person has taken and their average call time. These metrics hold a lot of weight due to their clarity of information and compatibility with other numbers on the board, however neither is a reflection of how customers are treated.

The structures of your operating model, and its regular policies, processes and procedures, are the riverbed that shapes your organisational culture, and because these tangible elements are often easier to understand and compare, our brains focus on them.

As neuroscientist Beau Lotto explains in his book *Deviate*, the human brain is designed to reduce uncertainty. In a complex and competitive work environment, our brain seeks an indication of its relative level of safety. It is then presented with an intangible and subjective message about customer satisfaction, and many more tangible and objective measures concerning call volumes and length of time on the phone. These are accompanied by equally clear targets, and we see how we are performing compared to peers in real-time on the screen. This is like taking a child to a buffet full of chocolate cakes and treats, but hiding a few carrot sticks in a back corner and expecting the child to choose the healthier option.

Understanding how your people experience their work-life is critical: what they focus on, what they worry about, and how different elements in their environment shape their decisions are all vital information for a leader. Habits form in the brain through repetition, and no colourful poster can outweigh the impact of systems, processes, rewards and regular actions.

Building alignment between culture and the operating model is a tough and constantly changing game. Leaders must get out of their offices and onto the floor to see what is happening, because you can't just set a strategy and hope - hope is a terrible plan. You must create, and be an active part of a continuous feedback loop where activity and emotions feed purposeful performance, and when divergence appears, you must address it.

Presta and Paying Attention To The Pain

Meeting Jim turned out to be a very interesting experience. After a brief call, when he seemed distracted and couldn't get off the phone quickly enough, we agreed to have a quick coffee early on Wednesday morning before he went to the factory.

"Thank you for taking the time to meet me, Jim. I can only imagine how intense things are for you at the moment. What time do you want us to wrap up so you can get back?" I asked, handing him the large flat white with three sugars he had asked for.

"Can we make it no more than ten minutes? I had a call in the middle of the night from my contact at the port saying there would be a delay on the next shipment arriving, so now we have to reschedule a full day's work and call our distributors. It will likely mean I'll be in the van again on the way home tonight making some of the special order deliveries." It wasn't yet seven in the morning, and Jim already looked exhausted.

"Are you okay, Jim? I don't want to dive into the details this morning, but you look pretty stretched." I asked, concerned about his health.

"To be honest, I don't have time to stop and think about myself. Every day seems to throw up new challenges, and I just have to keep putting out one fire after the next." Jim spoke with a sense of realisation and almost surprise as though he was only just realising how bad it was.

"In my experience, that can't last. I've been in these situations before, and either things change or people burn out and leave. I know about the time pressure, but what usually drives the pressure on you and your team?" I asked, moving closer to Jim to offer my support.

"It's a squeeze from all sides. We've got the sales team requesting more and more products - usually a lot of last-minute or one-off orders. At the same time, our suppliers struggle to keep up with the orders we put through. I get frustrated with phone calls from all sides, and we seem to be letting everyone down. We have pretty tight service agreements with our customers, and we've not been meeting them consistently for months." As Jim finished his sentence, his frustration seemed to fade into resignation.

"That must be disappointing for you and your people, Jim," I said as he seemed to relax a little, having been frantic when I had handed him the coffee just seconds earlier. "You know, one of the things I wanted to chat about was this meeting we've called for tomorrow for the leadership team." I paused to gauge his reaction.

Jim took a deep breath but didn't respond immediately.

"I can imagine, given the pressure, you may be a little concerned this will be a waste of time," I continued, and Jim nodded. "I want to reassure you that this meeting is designed to dig to the heart of these types of pressures and develop ways of alleviating them. I'm not sure if you'll agree, Jim, but I feel that these service agreements and processes you've all put in place are simply not working at the moment, but, because they're in place, everyone is focused on meeting them."

"We used to meet them at above ninety percent, but with the current supply situation, it's impossible," Jim said, showing my guess was on the mark.

"One of the challenges, I find, is that when things change rapidly outside an organisation, divisional leaders just work their teams harder instead of sitting back and thinking strategically about how they should respond," I replied, and noticed Jim had a smile on his face.

"You really think that Vanessa is going to break her contracts just to help out the production team?" Jim laughed. I had heard about Vanessa Matthews, the Head of Customers and Sales, from Rick. She was a recent hire from a large multinational, and had been seen as part of the reason for the surge in revenue in the group over the past twelve months.

"Jim, do you like football?" I asked, knowing he probably did as I had noticed the Manchester United bumper sticker on his car.

"Yeah, I played semi-professionally for a few years when I was younger," Jim said with a look of fond reminiscence.

"Me too. I remember in pre-season training, the coach would push us to run laps of the cricket field," I said to Jim who nodded, guessing what I was about to say. "After about five or six laps of sprinting and jogging, people would start to fall. I found for some guys it was their lungs - it was like they couldn't get enough air. For some, it was their legs; they just started to cramp up. Others, it wasn't their legs or lungs, it was heart rate - they simply couldn't maintain the effort." Jim tapped his legs, indicating this was where he'd struggled.

"You know what, Jim, it didn't matter which it was. Once some part of the system failed, you'd have to stop. Our coach wouldn't berate us or scream at us to keep going - first he'd ask which it was, what was hurting, and then he'd give us a set of exercises to work on to improve that area. Often it was swimming for the lungs, lunges and squats for the legs, and stair sprints for the heart rate. See, as a company you're a system all working together, so when one part breaks down, you all eventually fall."

"You're right. Sometimes I would try to run through the cramps, but it always ended badly!" Jim grimaced at the thought.

"So what I think we should explore as a leadership team is why we have issues, and what we have to do to improve as a team. We need to set up some new ways to work together, so we can get back on the field and bang in a few goals. We both know what will happen if we keep trying to run at this pace, don't we?"

Jim nodded, and said "All right, I get it. I'll be there. Just don't be surprised if there are a few fireworks!" He smiled like the Cheshire Cat from Alice in Wonderland, and I knew, given the dynamics I was seeing already, that the meeting was going to be both very important and pretty interesting.

Aligning Culture & Strategy

The Big Question & Actions

Does your operating model support the guiding principles you want in your culture?

- Identify the core elements of your operating model that people engage with regularly

- Analyse what these processes, targets and engagements feel like for your people

- Encourage your people to reflect regularly on how different meetings and interactions make them feel.

Part 3
Embedding guiding principles in culture

Chapter 5
Realigning
The Culture Flow

———

Highlights

- Our experiences shape how we perceive a culture through our actions
- If you want to shape culture, focus on shaping the things people do regularly
- Constantly assessing and adapting the operating model will ensure alignment as the world around you changes.

"If the rate of change on the outside exceeds the rate of change on the inside, the end is near."

Jack Welch

When elements of the operating model clash, they shape your culture in unforeseen ways, and the solution is not to roll out colourful new posters and bean bags. Too often this is just lipstick on a pig, and sometimes a small change to the very systems and processes that are creating the misalignment can be far more helpful.

The river will follow the riverbed, so we need to make sure the elements of the operating model flow in the direction we choose. For the sales team focused on their individual performances, a few simple tweaks made a dramatic change.

The first change we recommended was to the commission structure. Each team member was being paid a monthly commission based solely on their individual sales revenue. This financial incentive made up a substantial portion of their overall income, and was a key measure of performance.

So instead of their commission being purely the result of their sales, we changed that to 70% based on their sales and 30% based on the team's overall sales performance. The change was not instant, and there was some concern from people in the team - some contracts had to be adjusted, and the need to change explained in detail, but after a few months people had come to care about and support each other and their results. This aligned more with their desired principle of teamwork and celebrating success, as now they had to work together for shared results.

We also changed the structure of the sales meetings. The manager of the team now opened meetings with a team view of performance and collective tracking. Then threats and opportunities for the group were discussed, so that sales meetings focused on the team rather than individuals. One-on-one meetings coached and supported individual performance, allowing team meetings to be more collective.

Even the way team members approached prospecting began to reshape naturally when, rather than each salesperson building up a bank of future clients, they started to share them across the team. When someone was struggling to get enough new clients to meet their goals, teammates offered some of their prospects, and even their conversations were more client-focused.

Aligning Culture & Strategy

The team began to look at their prospect lists from a customer perspective, and ask around the room who knew the most about different industries, and geographic or demographic groups.

The focus changed to team conversion rates instead of individual successes as they discussed who could best help a potential client, instead of trying to land every client. So they started working as a team, and not as a group of mercenaries, and their leader supported them with guiding principles and conversation rather than just processes and KPIs.

Throughout the first year, there were a lot of changes and challenges, and some of the team chose to leave for a more individualistic workplace. But the persistent focus on aligning behaviours and processes to the guiding principles paid off, and the team became the number one sales team in their industry, had the highest customer satisfaction, and delivered excellent financial results.

Constantly evaluating and reshaping your operating model to support the culture you want and need is a vital role of every leader. No matter how well you design a process, system or structure, as the world changes and evolves at some point your A-grade process becomes obsolete. It is their relentless focus on constantly enhancing and improving that enables companies like Toyota and Amazon to adapt to the many challenges they face.

Adjusting Presta's Sails

Arriving at Presta's head office, I was a little surprised that Rick had not answered my calls since we had agreed to have a chat before the session. I was worried something might have come up, and as I walked into reception, I could hear heated discussions from down the hallway, and Katrina, the receptionist, looked at me, blushing with embarrassment.

"Rick's asked me to take you through to the boardroom, and help you set up. Can I get you a coffee?" she asked as she ushered me away from the clearly audible arguments.

I looked at my watch as I paced around the Presta boardroom. We were scheduled for a 9:00 am start, and it was 8:59. As I sat there on my own, I thought about Jim, and wondered if they would all feel too busy for this meeting, but to my surprise Jim was the first person to come in.

"Hello, Jim, great to see you again." I reached out to shake his hand, and noticed the expression on his face was a blend of kindness and concern.

"Are you sure you're ready for this?" Jim asked.

"Why do you say that?" Clearly, Jim had some inside information I wasn't privy to.

"Rick has been fighting fires to keep this meeting alive since late yesterday. There were emails flying around at midnight trying to get it cancelled. Stefan was complaining he has an audit to respond to, and Vanessa flat out told everyone that she thought it was a waste of time," Jim said quietly as he leaned across the large table, his eyebrows dancing with excitement.

Stefan Martin was the group's Financial Officer, and I had spoken to him briefly during the week, but he hadn't mentioned any concerns about the meeting. Vanessa had not answered any of my calls to her yesterday. This was going to be a fun session!

At 9:05 am, Rick and Stefan came in, Rick looking exhausted. Stefan smiled sheepishly in my direction, and before I could say anything Vanessa stormed in, threw her notebook on the table, looked at me and raised a hand in acknowledgement.

"Hi, you must be Daniel. I'm Vanessa," she said briskly.

As I smiled and nodded at Vanessa, the final member of the team, Sam Stevenson, came in quietly and sat down. Sam was the Head of People, Culture & Risk. We had not yet met, but Rick had mentioned that Sam was far more focused on risk than on people.

Sam had been with the organisation for more than a decade, and while well-liked didn't appear to have the respect of the team. They all settled into their chairs, Rick looked at me as if to suggest we were ready. I stood up and kicked things off.

"Before we kick off, I want you to grab a piece of paper and a pen," I said to the now silent room. "I want you to write down answers to the following questions. These are just your personal answers - no need for discussion just yet.

Question one, out of ten, and ten being the best you can expect, how would you rate the current culture in your team?

Question two, what is the most important thing your team needs to change to improve this score?

Question three, when I asked these questions, whom did you think of?"

Vanessa stared at me. "I don't understand. You're asking about our teams? Do you mean the individuals in our team?" she snapped.

"Yeah, I don't really have a team," Sam said quietly.

"Interesting," I said, looking at the others to see how they felt. "What did each of you have for question three? Jim?" I pointed at Jim, given his friendly nature.

"I thought of my production leads and project managers. They are the people I work most closely with. I scored them a five for the moment, and think we need more resources to improve," he said confidently.

"I thought of my accounting team. There are only three of us all up, but I think we're functioning well. I gave us an eight. I think once we implement a new finance system we'll be closer to nine or ten," Stefan said.

"Vanessa, were you thinking of your team as your direct reports?" I asked, noticing her expression had changed.

"Yeah, I was, but I think I see where you're going." Vanessa smiled. "We don't see ourselves as a team. This is a leadership team, and yet when we think of our teams we immediately think about the people who report to us. Rick, what score did you give?" Vanessa asked, looking at Rick who was grinning.

"I need to change my answer to question two. I was thinking of this leadership team as my team, and had given us a two out of ten." I suspected the rough morning meant Rick wasn't holding back. "Initially I had thought it was our strategy that needed to change, or maybe we even needed a restructure to refit roles and responsibilities, but I've realised that it's the lack of clear, guiding principles in the way we lead that's our problem. In fact, I think the big problem is my leadership." The room fell silent as he paused and looked at his notebook.

"This is meant to be a leadership team but, on reflection, our meetings are more like a bunch of politicians coming together to fight for their constituents. I often feel like a referee not a leader, and that's my fault. I need to change." Rick turned back a few pages in his notebook.

"At Presta, we take ownership and follow through. We make things right when they're wrong. We support the home team and look out for each other. We embrace the hard questions that push us to improve," Rick read out, pointing to the list in his notebook with his pen.

Aligning Culture & Strategy

"Sorry, where did these statements come from?" asked Sam leaning across the table.

"Daniel and I started chatting last week, and went through our values, and since then I've been working on a new set of values that I think we should implement. Actually, no. I don't want to call them our values. I want them to be our guiding principles, the set of commitments that we and everyone else in the business need to uphold." As Rick said this, I could see how much his confidence in this process had increased.

Stefan jumped in, "But we did the values thing not that long ago. I don't think we need new values or principles or words. I think we need…"

"What are they?" Rick interrupted Stefan.

"What, the values?" asked Stefan, sitting back in his chair. "Umm, I think respect was one. Performance?"

"Exactly. What we have today is an unmemorable laundry list that people can't remember," Rick replied. "I think we need to make guiding principles that are clearer and more direct."

"Let's just pause for a second," I jumped in, making sure we didn't get too far ahead of ourselves. "It sounds like, Rick, you would agree that this leadership team is not working effectively as a team. What does everyone else think?"

"It's true, I don't think we work well together," Jim agreed as other heads nodded.

"Great. At least we know where we need to start. This team is the most important team in the whole organisation. This is the centre, where decisions are made that shape the way the whole business works, yet we are not working together. While you may need to review your strategy, particularly given the current climate, you probably need to start with how you want to work together. What are the principles that will guide your decision-making? That wall out there," I gestured to the wall in reception covered in the colourful words, "is undeniably full of nice words, but what we need in this room are a set of clear principles to guide us."

The room fell silent, and Vanessa was the first to speak up. "I totally agree. Jim, we've been butting heads for the past few weeks." She pointed at Jim who was sitting opposite her. "And things have not really improved. In fact, I worry about our teams gossiping and whining about each other. I don't think that's their fault, or that they can even fix that. That's really up to us, isn't it?"

"Spot on, Vanessa," Jim replied, accepting her olive branch generously. "And we need to get on the same page first. Then we need to support each other in how we go forward. I think having a principle like 'support each other in the home team' would make this clearer to everyone - me included!"

With this, Rick stood up and walked to the whiteboard. In a thick black marker, he wrote Presta GUIDING PRINCIPLES, and below that the four draft principles he had given:

- We take ownership and follow through.
- We make things right when they're wrong.
- We support the home team and look out for each other.
- We embrace the hard questions that push us to improve.

"Should it be 'make things right' or 'do the right thing'?" Sam murmured from down the table.

"Let's not get hung up on specific words when what we want to focus on is meaning. A great way of analysing and clarifying the meaning each of you understands from these principles is to put them to the test. Let's dive into some of the issues you're facing now, and use them to discuss possible ways forward," I said, not wanting to go down the rabbit hole of finding exactly the right words. "Jim and Vanessa, can we start with one of your issues?"

For the next three hours, we discussed the business's most serious difficulties. They used the guiding principles frequently as a reflection tool and, on most issues, this allowed them to find common ground and plot a path forward.

There were a few more testing topics that we agreed needed more work, and I labelled them 'Do Next' and posted them on a board. For each agreed step forward, we added specific actions on a board marked 'Do Now', and each was assigned someone to take it forward in alignment with the take ownership and follow-through principles.

When the clock struck half-past twelve, we called it a day and picked up our notebooks.

"Before we leave today, may I first say thank you? I know some of you are under immense stress, and half a day is a big ask. Give me one more rating out of ten before you leave, how would you rate this session?" I asked the group.

"Easy, ten!" Jim called out, pleased to help with immediate pressures.

"I'd say a nine" added Vanessa. "We certainly made impressive progress."

"Nine from me too," Stefan agreed. "I'm really happy to have more precision on some of these issues I didn't really recognise before. That helps me understand some of the numbers better."

Rick looked at Sam, who clearly wanted to be the last to announce a score.

"I don't know. I'd probably say five. I think we spent a lot of time talking about problems we already knew existed, and I don't really want to go through another process to change the values," Sam said, staring at the whiteboard.

"Well, I found it really useful," said Rick. "It's the first time that I've felt the issues spinning around in my head have been shared out loud. I know how hard you worked on the values last time, Sam, and there was a lot of heated debate and discussion, even on which word would be which colour. But I truly believe that at a time like this, when we have so many issues, we need to be clear on how we work together as a leadership team."

"I would have agreed with you yesterday, Sam," Vanessa said, "and actually even when I walked in this morning I expected this to be a total waste of time. But do you realise today is the first time Jim and I have actually talked about ways to work together? I mean really thought it through. On reflection, I know that sounds terrible, but we can't change the past. I really feel these guiding principles have helped us to hold a better conversation."

Jim and Stefan both nodded in agreement, and as everyone left the room Rick leaned on the table wearing a large smile. "Do you hear that?" he asked me, cupping his left ear.

"Hear what?" I asked.

"They're chatting!" Rick replied. He was right, I could hear Jim, Stefan and Vanessa talking to each other as they walked down the hallway.

"I've not heard them talk like that in months. They usually rush out head down and on their phones. I think we had some breakthroughs today." Rick smiled again. "I'll have a chat with Sam later today. There's a bit of history there, but I feel like we're on a better path already."

I shook Rick's hand, and made my way to my car with my lists and notes ready to be developed into an output report for the team. It had been a long morning, and, while we had set out the foundations for Presta to rebuild their leadership team, right now I needed lunch!

The Big Question & Actions

Does your leadership team meeting express the guiding principles you want to implant in the organisation?

- Analyse your leadership team systematically to ensure you are holding critical conversations

- Make changes to the way you interact to reinforce guiding principles in your leadership team

- Reinforce your guiding principles in your leadership team first, to ensure they are leader-driven.

Part 4
Clarity, Empathy & Leadership

Chapter 6
Purposeful Performance

———

- Clarity is critical to ensure that you are providing your people with a set of consistent expectations that they understand

- Empathy is vital to awaken curiosity and obtain better feedback on how your organisational culture is developing

- Leadership skills should be embedded across the organisation, not just in people with a title.

"The leader is one who, out of the clutter, brings simplicity ... out of discord, harmony ... and out of difficulty, opportunity."

Albert Einstein

The Aligned Organisation Model shows that when your values, culture, strategy and operating model are all aligned, organisations deliver Purposeful Performance. This leads to increased employee engagement and commitment, improved customer and client outcomes and satisfaction, and more consistent financial performance. When your organisation aligns tangible and intangible elements all the way from planning through execution, this creates the environment for more concrete and sustainable results.

However, this is unlikely to be a static position. While things may be harmonious internally today, the world outside is constantly changing, and this will impact your organisation. This is in large part why we see so many wonderfully laid plans, and millions spent on management consultants, failing to deliver in the long term - and rehashed plans that worked before not leading to their previous success.

As Mike Tyson said, "Everybody has a plan until they get punched in the mouth." While it is unlikely that your competitors will walk into your office and beat you, up there are a million sophisticated ways to bring down your best plans, and if you are successful there are a lot of motivated groups seeking to do this.

To sustain success, your organisation needs to be able to constantly monitor what is changing, re-evaluate this against your strategic vision, and, most importantly, take appropriate action to rebuild the alignment needed for purposeful performance.

The three critical capabilities your organisation needs to be sustainably successful and deliver on purposeful performance are: Clarity, Empathy and Leadership.

Clarity

Communication is a very complex process. We do it all the time in so many ways - from when we are born - and take it for granted, but let's break it down. Inside your head, through a complex pattern of neurons firing in specific timings, you form what you perceive as an idea. This idea is the distillation of millions of related and tangential, conflicting and even impossible ideas. Think of all of that swirling like a cloud inside your head -and this specific idea represents that complex cloud in a single thought that you consciously conceive.

Now you search for words and language to represent this complex cloud, and find a collection of words that seem to describe it best. You transmit these words and associated bodily movements in a display we call communication to a person who actually observes only part of this.

They have to interpret what you mean based on their observations, which they feed into a thunderous storm of ideas in their own mind. You hope that the ideas in your head are replicated in theirs, and that your communication has been accurately interpreted and understood. Simple, right?

Hardly! Add to this transaction millions of other bits of information bombarding both brains. Your brain receives around 11 million bits of data a second, and these noises and body movements are only a tiny percentage. When you put together random noises, distractions, internal factors of mood, hunger, temperature and, of course, existing ideas, beliefs and assumptions, it's a wonder we ever agree about anything.

This is why clarity is such a simple term with such a profound impact on alignment and performance. When you develop an intricate strategy requiring large groups of people to coordinate in specific ways within a complex, volatile and ever-changing environment, not much needs to go wrong for this to fall short of your expectations, so that clarity on the strategy is of the utmost importance.

Similarly, when setting out guiding principles you need to be clear about what they mean. Integrity is a value cited by many organisations, but does this mean we should all make ethical judgements and only act in accordance with them? Or does it mean we comply with the legal regulations and obligations that apply to our organisation? There's a saying "just because it's legal doesn't mean it's ethical", but perhaps it does in some organisations. Both definitions of integrity have very different implications for behaviours and outcomes.

If half your team makes an ethical decision never to invest in projects that could have a subjectively assessed environmental impact, whereas the other half is happily investing in perfectly legal but environmentally flawed projects in the coal mining or fast fashion industries, what does your organisation really stand for? Both teams could argue they are acting with integrity, but which is correct? Which aligns with the intention of the leadership team when it was chosen as your organisational value?

Without clarity, your people are likely to become misaligned - either strategically or culturally - and this will weaken your organisation. Inconsistency frustrates customers - fingers point and trust is eroded. Then it becomes harder to attract talent, and people are asked to do more with less. A downward spiral misalignment can be fatal.

Here are three tips to help increase the clarity of both your strategy and guiding principles:

1) Share Stories

Teams often spend countless hours debating, discussing and exploring scenarios before building a strategy. Analysts may be engaged to create elaborate databases of information; post-it notes cover the walls; heated discussions overwhelm the boardroom table; and consultants are commissioned to construct a huge PowerPoint pack full of graphs and chevrons detailing the plan.

After all these attempts to create a grand plan, what cascades down to the people who actually have to deliver this strategy is often far less comprehensive. In fact the strategy is often broken down into factual instructions, processes and KPIs/OKRs that, in isolation, leave employees scratching their heads and wondering what all the fuss was about.

Professor Jennifer Aaker of Stanford's research has shown that stories are remembered up to 22 times more than facts alone. If I say Three Little Pigs, not only do you probably know the story, but also the meaning behind it – and that's in just three words.

Human brains love stories, so make sure your strategy and guiding principles are expressed in living stories, and give real life examples of how your strategy will affect the lives of customers and stakeholders. Share stories of the expectations you have in terms of guiding principles and behaviours, and describe your strategy and guiding principles in narrative form as much as possible, rich with emotions and human experiences that your people can relate to. We know that makes them clearer, and easier to share and far more memorable than facts alone.

2) Ask Questions

Every day people are bombarded with thousands of messages, and between phone calls, social media, meetings, employee discussions, external news and hundreds of emails, everyone needs to constantly sort through this flood of daily information to work out what's important and what isn't, what should be remembered and what can be ignored. This is no easy task.

Sometimes leaders assume that anything they say will cut through this noise and be heard and listened to. Leaders are in a position of authority after all, and people are supposed to hang on their every word, but this is both naive and dangerously wrong. With so many competing priorities, it is easy for busy people to feel swamped, so a long email describing your strategy may just be scanned and filed into a 'read later' folder, never to be seen again.

Even in a meeting - any meeting - devices beep and vibrate with requests diverting people's attention from what they are doing to the mountain of work they will need to climb as soon as they leave. You may get a nod of agreement when you ask if people understand, despite their not really grasping much of what was said, let alone applying it to their work.

I'm not suggesting people intentionally ignore what their leaders are saying; they're often just too busy. So one of the simplest yet most effective ways to ensure they have understood your plans is to ask them questions:

- What do you think this will mean for your team?
- What changes do you think we will need to make for this to work?
- What challenges do you see this presenting?
- What do you need from me to make this work?

Simple questions like these are a great way to confirm comprehension, deepen understanding and help move from ideas into action plans ready to implement.

3) Repeat Often

If your school was anything like mine, then reciting your times tables was common practice. As boring as that was, now if someone asks me what seven times eight is, in my mind a little voice from a distant classroom chants "seven eights are fifty-six".

Repetition is one of the fundamental ways the brain creates and stores memory. While it doesn't necessarily build understanding, the constant firing of certain neural clusters in specific patterns strengthens connections and supports information retention. From times tables to song lyrics, and from old passwords to advertising slogans, the things we hear and say often stick in our heads long after their utility has faded.

Why then do many organisations spend a lot of time, money and effort in rolling out a strategic vision, but fail to repeat it? Sometimes you feel like a broken record if you have to repeat the same thing at every meeting - like one of those annoying late-night television adverts that seems to be on a loop.

In fact you feel like this because the connections and memories are already strong in your mind - but that doesn't mean other people have retained them. There's a good chance that the first few times they've heard you say something, they were so busy thinking about everything else going on that they weren't actually listening.

When you develop and disseminate a new strategy and set of guiding principles, you are trying to align the ideas people have on a range of different topics in a single direction. Imagine each person believing the

Aligning Culture & Strategy

company is heading in a certain direction, and every action and decision they have made in the past has reinforced their belief.

Now you come along and talk about a new direction. Even if they listen the first time, it won't be enough to change those embedded neural pathways.

You need to repeat, repeat, repeat. Build a consistent set of messages that people hear all the time until they become a mantra in their minds. This is critical to planting your strategy and guiding principles, because, in the hustle and bustle of 'busywork', our brains fall back on deeply embedded ideas to make decisions - not some document or webpage we saw once a few months ago.

To add variety and deepen understanding, each time you repeat your mantra, add different stories. Share stories that are as relevant to the specific audience as possible, and add thoughts from different perspectives to help bring more colour to the ideas. But don't forget to repeat.

You will know when you have repeated your strategy and guiding principles enough, because you'll hear other people using the same words. This is when you really start to create a strong sense of "The way we do things around here."

A Final Thought On Clarity...

If you're in a middle management role and feel that, while all the above makes sense, you don't really understand the strategy or guiding principles well enough, then you have to ask questions. It's your responsibility as a people leader to create clarity for your people. It's also your responsibility as a member of the organisation to seek clarity where you don't feel it exists. If your people are seeking clarity from you, it's vital you seek clarity upwards too. It is not the people who ask questions who create problems; it's the passive, misaligned majority who cause the most pain.

Empathy

Before you assume this section will be all warm and fluffy, let me clarify what I mean by empathy. Today we are bombarded with data, spreadsheets and dashboards that constantly inform us of our measurable, tangible performance. Some leaders I know are able to analyse their performance in real-time with live dashboards flashing numbers and graphs across the screen. In this way, we have a better understanding of performance than ever before.

Based on my experience, many leaders have lost touch with their people. They get up-to-date and detailed reports on sales volumes, but only vague and irregular feedback about what their targets mean, and if they are in alignment with the company's guiding principles. In a world full of so many different influences and consequences, empathy is the ability to understand other people: why they do what they do, and how our activities affect them - for good or for bad.

I use the term empathy because I want to emphasise not only the need for us to build understanding, but that we should expect this understanding to involve complex ideas that are deeply nuanced and personal. Recognising your influence on people does more than simply give you a relative scorecard to observe. Empathy creates a more powerful outcome: connection.

As important as clarity of guiding principles, without empathy our guiding principles and ethical decisions may lack the right useful context. Our environment and experiences constantly shape and reshape our minds, and there are two major factors to consider here: Mental Models and Attention.

Our Mental Models are the frameworks that we use to assign meaning and value to the world around us. Our brains are constantly bombarded with millions of bits of data that they need to interpret to navigate and make decisions. Some models are relatively universal: upturned corners of the mouth with a slight clenching of muscles around the eyes is generally called a mental model for a smile. But universal models are much more of a rarity than we might think, and we often overestimate how common our models are.

A good example is blowing your nose: in many western countries, it is perfectly acceptable to pull a piece of cloth out of your pocket in front of other people, blow an assortment of particles from your nose into this cloth, and then put it back in your pocket. In Japan, this would be seen as very rude, even disgusting.

Speaking loudly at the dinner table is frowned upon in some cultures, and the norm in others. Using your fingers to eat food, tipping a waiter, touching someone with your feet, even speaking to someone while looking them straight in the eye... all of these may be seen as perfectly normal or totally unacceptable.

The key point here is that none of these actions in themselves has any real positive or negative intention nor implication. It is only when it is interpreted by people using their existing mental models that it suddenly has any meaning or value.

This is why actively practising empathy is so important. In the Empathy Process I created, the first step to master is to become Consciously Curious. I coined this term to refer to the exercise of bringing awareness to the fact that you have mental models you would normally use to make sense of a situation, but that you are consciously parking these models and any judgement so as to remain open and curious.

An important point here: this is incredibly easy to say and difficult to practise. Your brain defaults to making judgements instantly using the least amount of energy, and it does this by referencing your mental models. In *Thinking Fast And Slow*, Nobel Prize-winning psychologists, Daniel Kahneman and Amos Tversky describe two ways we think: *System 1* and *System 2*. While we can think about things slowly, questioning deeply and exploring ideas with curiosity, we mostly rely on *System 1*. They detail many situations where this type of fast and efficient judgement is used regularly, but turns out to be easily fooled or misled.

"*System 1* is highly adept in one form of thinking — it automatically and effortlessly identifies causal connections between events, sometimes even when the connection is spurious," Kahneman and Tversky explain. We automatically use our mental models to make sense of a situation, and assume the result is accurate.

Ancient humans didn't take time to ponder all that often - they had to act immediately as it was a matter of life and death. There was no time to wonder whether a tiger ready to pounce was rustling in the bushes or a bush turkey scratching for grubs. It was better to make a judgement and act - there weren't that many possibilities, and you had to make a quick decision based on experience. They relied on the more energy efficient *System 1*, and it served them well.

The level of complexity we have to deal with today has exploded. We are all dealing with significantly more complex situations and, even more challenging, with many, many more diverse human interactions. Where ancient humans were surrounded by a few people who shared many of their lived experiences, today we are surrounded by hundreds of people who are like us in some ways, and completely different in others.

This diversity is simultaneously our greatest advantage and challenge. We are surrounded by so many fixed and diverse views, old and new ideas, and brilliant sparks of potential inspiration, but these can also seem frustratingly unfamiliar and threatening. When we are busy working, or deeply focused on a certain set of objectives, actions or measures, our ability to consider alternative ideas and explore different perspectives broadly may be constrained.

While people who go to the beach regularly can easily spot the telltale signs of a dangerous rip tide, people with no experience may wade into the calm water only to be sucked out into the ocean. Similarly, people in a team focused on specific results may be very skilled at seeing the processes of delivering these results, but totally miss the important signs that others are experiencing unfavourable outcomes.

Here are three tips to help you and your team to develop greater empathy. Specifically, these will help your people to identify the impact your team is having on both internal and external stakeholders.

1) Questions as a Reflex

There are two specific parts of our brain that leap into action whenever we are confronted with something new. Our Ventral Striatum starts to assign a sense of value, assessing whether this is this useful, or favourable and something I like. At the same time, the Amygdala determines if this new input is a threat, or dangerous and should we be wary? These two very important parts of our brain are vital for our survival. We need them to make judgements on the usefulness or danger of everything we encounter.

While these systems are crucial, they can also make us overly judgmental. Our brains almost automatically and instantly assess every new opinion, idea, thought or discussion in our daily lives as positive or negative. Our ancient brains are for or against before we've even allowed our more sophisticated cognitive processes to form an impression, and this is why fostering curiosity and empathy is so important.

Training yourself and your team to develop a question reflex is a great way of interrupting this automatic judgement system. As a leader, you can learn this skill by getting into the habit of asking simple and easily repeatable questions like:

- That's interesting, can you tell me more?
- What else do we know about this?
- How can we understand this further?

Getting into the habit of asking a question provides a number of immediate benefits. Firstly, genuine interest in them reassures people and makes them feel safer, and more open to sharing their ideas. When we suggest a new idea to someone and their first reaction is to pass judgement, particularly a negative one, it makes our Amygdala fire, igniting our threat response, and possibly influencing any wish to communicate further.

Secondly, asking a question as your first response buys your brain time to recognise your initial reaction, resist your instincts to judge, and deliberate more consciously. You may think you do this automatically, but try this little exercise for a few weeks: whenever you disapprove, simply pause and ask a question like the ones above. Then write down what stimulus caused the initial reaction, and how it felt. When you've thought about it, review your earliest reactions against your more considered view after the deeper exploration. And let me know the results!

Thirdly, and most importantly, asking questions helps you gather and absorb far more information. While our automatic judgements are fast and efficient, they rarely take the complexities of our world into account. By pausing and practising curiosity, we can often access additional inputs. Much like in a television court case, the more we are able to dive into the details, uncover facts, explore motives, and understand different perspectives, the more information we can assess to truly understand a situation so as to make better decisions.

2) Ask for Disagreement

Set a time in every discussion for people to disagree with the emerging ideas, even their own. It will be hard at first, and I highly recommend bringing this in to the team slowly or using a skilled facilitator either from within your company or an external provider. Creating a time where everyone is looking for a way of breaking from their emerging thoughts and going against the grain is incredibly powerful.

Alfred P. Sloan, CEO of General Motors in the mid-1900s, once said to his leadership team:

"If we are all in agreement on the decision - then I propose we postpone further discussion of this matter until our next meeting to give ourselves time to develop disagreement and perhaps gain some understanding of what the decision is all about."

Full agreement in a group may be a sign of worrying patterns of behaviour, as sometimes people agree due to a lack of understanding, as in I'm not really across this topic, so I'll just agree and hope everyone else knows what they're talking about. Or sometimes people agree for relationship reasons - I like Bill and I want him to like me, so I'll just go with the flow. Or for social reasons: Everyone seems to agree with this, and I don't want to be the odd one out.

Too often, most of us aren't even sure why we're agreeing. It may feel easier than disagreeing, or more risky professionally to, literally, stand up and speak out.

But there is a risk in agreeing too quickly, so try allotting a designated time for everyone to contest ideas, their own and others'. Encourage and support people to actively think out of their comfort zones and explore the situation fully.

3) Ask How It Feels

There is a long-held myth that Peter Drucker once said "What gets measured gets managed," meaning that we should focus our attention on the aspects of organisations that can be measured. Firstly, the Peter Drucker Institute denies he ever said this, but, more importantly, we know from our own lives that there are a lot of vitally important things that we can't reliably measure.

How nice does a hug feel?

How much do you love your partner?

How satisfying is your favourite meal when you're really hungry?

None of these is particularly easy, nor that useful, to turn into metrics, but they certainly matter. We can get so caught up with the spreadsheets, reports, visual dashboards and other numbers that dominate our minds, that we lose sight of, and insights from, some of these intangible elements.

Asking people to describe how something feels encourages them to step out of a purely factual/numbers frame, and into more intuitive and emotion-based thought processes. Encourage your team members to put the figures aside for a moment, and step into the world of a customer, colleague, stakeholder, regulator or journalist - how might they feel about this?

As a little bonus, curiosity and empathy in a team can become contagious. Much like other behaviours, asking questions and exploring ideas can become a cultural habit, and a strong antidote to the common issues of false assumptions, hidden agendas and offline politics that plague too many busy teams when it comes to really understanding the situations they face, and making decisions that go beyond just short-term impact.

A Final Thought On Empathy...

Empathy is a formidable skill, but having a greater understanding of your influence on a variety of stakeholder groups is a critical one. How can you know you are delivering the results you intend if you don't understand the impact you have? It's so easy to get caught up in the numbers and forget, and we don't run organisations to make spreadsheets. We run organisations to affect people's lives.

If we can't see the broader impact of our actions, it is possible - indeed likely - that we will make impulsive or short-sighted decisions. Empathy has many benefits, including enabling greater perspective for more purposeful results.

Leadership

When reviewing case studies of organisational failings, it is easy to get caught up in the search for a sinister actor, a mastermind who has plotted carefully to deliberately deceive, defraud and destroy. We look at the Wolf of Wall Street Jordan Belfort, Ponzi mastermind Bernie Madoff, and Enron CEO Jeff Skilling, and think they are the type of criminal to be afraid of - narcissists hell-bent on self-gratification without a care for anyone else.

This is a bit like fear of sharks though. The chance of being killed by accidental poisoning is roughly 200,000 times greater than by a shark, but do you read the back of each packet of food carefully before buying it? Our fear centre lights up depending on how we imagine a risk, but is poor at considering its actual probability. You can visualise those massive jaws of a great white with rows of razor-sharp teeth, but you can't imagine a bad tub of yogurt causing your demise.

Similarly, organisations are on the lookout for the big killers, and sometimes miss the thousand little cuts which are bleeding us dry. The biggest challenge is an erosion of cultural and strategic alignment - not a big bang, a slow rot.

Culture is formed by the million little things we do. We so often focus our attention on big, shiny objects, but the little things really do add up. Your brain is flooded by 11 million bits of data a second as the different sensory cells in every part of your body send it signals. But the conscious brain can only process around 50 signals a second - that is no typo - 50 out of 11 million, or 0.0005% of all the signals.

We don't know how many of these signals our subconscious brain attends to, although it must be a larger number. For instance, we take some exercise, and suddenly realise our heart rate has increased, capillaries in our face have opened, allowing more blood to the surface to release heat, and we start to perspire. None of this is consciously controlled, is it?

Our subconscious is constantly scanning inputs from our environment, and it sets off emotional and physiological responses based on the level of potential or perceived safety and threat. It listens to comments and assesses them as positive or negative, and judges friends or foes by the look on people's faces as it unceasingly gauges the world around us, so that we feel without being fully conscious of feeling.

For this reason, culture is influenced by absolutely everyone in an organisation. People at the top do indeed have a great impact, mainly due to the large number of major decisions they make and their flow-on effects, but they are not alone - everyone in an organisation influences culture in everything they do.

This is why the concept of implanting leadership within an organisation means much more than just training the C-suite. While good leaders build teams, great leaders build leaders. Leadership should not just be seen as a noun — to lead is a verb, and represents the actions people take, the decisions they make, the way they behave, and how they treat the people around them. Culture is shaped by the influence of leaders - and everyone can be a leader.

Embedding leadership is not easy though. In certain ways you will feel you are fighting the natural hierarchical structure - something many people enjoy doing. Here are three practical tips for implanting leadership in your team, and making everyone a custodian of the culture:

1) Don't accept apathy

Of all the traits that leaders should look out for, apathy is close to the top of the list. When people are upset and frustrated, it can sometimes be a sign that they really care and are passionate about your organisation. But the apathetic - who seem to drag themselves into work and are totally disengaged when they are there - are the people you need to be more concerned about.

Their lack of enthusiasm and passion leaves everyone with a sense of disappointment - like Eeyore in the Winnie-the-Pooh books, this attitude sucks the life out of your culture, so if you want leaders in your team, you cannot tolerate apathy.

This may seem odd, but attitudes we turn a blind eye to are attitudes we accept. Allowing apathy in a team is you as the leader signalling that this is okay - and says that in many ways, you too are apathetic.

The people in your team who first step up to the leadership plate will be passionate about the cause, and little smothers their enthusiasm more than perceived encouragement of apathy. If you want flowers to grow, you must weed, fertilise and water them with care. Your leaders just won't grow if they are stifled by apathy.

2) Ask for Hard Feedback

Sitting down to a few beers after work with my colleagues one day, the discussion turned to the way our boss was running the team, and they vented some of their frustration. It wasn't a positive conversation, and they were scathing about our manager, saying his instructions were muddled, his motivation absent, and our team meetings boring and the worst hour of the week.

What struck me the next day at our team meeting was that everyone seemed fine as all their frustration had faded into apathy. No one said a thing, and I realised things were not as bad as I had thought the night before - they were much worse. Not only did they not like our boss, but they didn't trust him enough to tell him so. It was this lack of feedback that would finally destroy his leadership.

Feedback is one of the most natural ways we acquire knowledge: we act, and our nervous system responds with a message that is sent to our brain, which decides whether it is positive, negative or neutral. This crude system is how we learn. Eat chocolate, and it tastes good. Step on a piece of Lego, and it is painful. Your brain learns: more chocolate and don't walk on Lego.

However, feedback rarely rises. Like my colleagues, many people are happy to share their thoughts with their peers, but not with the boss. That's like you placing your hand on a hot stove, and your pain sensors telling your friends while you remain oblivious, and just wonder where that funny smell is coming from.

If you want to build a leadership culture, ask everyone for feedback. Honest feedback on your performance as their leader will help you as people tell you things that you don't see, and challenge you in ways you haven't thought of, which develops your ability to lead.

And if you welcome and praise their feedback, you'll develop an even more powerful benefit for your team. If your team gets better at giving you feedback, they'll also get better at giving and receiving feedback from each other. This is the essence of a leadership culture: being able to hold difficult conversations, open conversations, and to call out things you don't agree with. Leadership includes being able to disagree without being disagreeable, and to challenge where there is any possible doubt.

Growing your leadership capability requires active challenges from everyone. You must be the catalyst by asking for direct feedback and accepting it with grace and interest when it comes.

3) Recognise Leadership Behaviours

Courage is not the absence of fear; it is action in the face of fear - a strength shared by great leaders across history and geography. From Aristotle to Mandela, and from Mark Twain to Martin Luther King Jr, courage has always been recognised as a key characteristic in the role of active leadership. Those who have the courage to stand up will become leaders.

It takes great courage to push against strong currents, and it is dangerous to speak up when others remain silent, to challenge when others submit, and to state that something may be wrong when everyone else seems to think it's right. Although many people will know they should do something, only a few will have the courage to act.

This courage is therefore a seed that needs to be carefully nourished and fostered if you want leadership to expand inside your organisation. When people speak up, challenge, and push against the grain, it is vital that you support them both vocally and publicly, and that everyone knows you do.

There is a caveat to this though - you have to support them even when they are wrong, their idea doesn't work, or their initiative fails. One reason we stop challenging and questioning is that many of us have had the experience of being wrong. The moment you thought you'd caught your teacher out only to feel the ridicule of your classmates when you're proven wrong is a feeling of isolation and shame we don't recover from quickly.

It's this fear of being wrong that stops people from speaking up and trying new things, but the reality is, all of us will be wrong some of the time - not every initiative succeeds. We don't need them all to be winners, but we do need a constant flow of new and challenging ideas to try to lead to the successes. Speaking up and being wrong is not such a bad thing, whereas not speaking up and being right may be fatal.

In the hours leading up to the Challenger space rocket launch, engineers were concerned that critical pieces of the rocket could not withstand the weather conditions. However, after so many delays and so much pressure from stakeholders, they said nothing. With the whole world watching, the parts failed, and 73 seconds after lift-off, Challenger broke apart killing all seven astronauts on board.

A speak-up culture needs leaders to encourage and reward challenging and speaking up, irrespective of the outcome. If one dissenting voice ensures everyone has really questioned their own thinking, it is an advantage to the whole group. A leader must encourage all the voices and behaviours that create a culture of constructive challenge.

When you see these behaviours, acknowledge them. Get into the habit of thanking people for their questions. Thank them for calling out risks. Thank them for airing their concerns. Don't wait to see if they are valid or not - that will eventually become obvious. Thank them regardless, in order to breed leadership from within.

A Final Thought On Leadership

Leadership is one of the most difficult and essential elements to build in your organisation. This is why we focus on, not just the intangible factors, but also how to develop leadership into the operating rhythm of the team - and systems, processes and routines are important ways to foster leadership, as they guide efficient and effective function.

We created a simple system for one of our clients to set standards and recognise behaviours. Their leadership team now assesses everyone in the organisation regularly, not only on KPIs but also on observed behaviours. They use a tick-dash-cross rating system, and each month they ask as a team if every member of the organisation has demonstrated behaviours aligned with the group's guiding principles.

In quarterly strategic review sessions, every member of the organisation is listed on a whiteboard, including the leadership team and CEO, and then a frank and open discussion is held, asking if they are living the guiding principles. Everyone on the list gets a tick if it's agreed that they have consistently displayed behaviours that align, a dash if they sometimes align, and a cross if they misalign. When members of the leadership team disagree on a rating, they have an open conversation and work through examples until everyone agrees.

Initially this was very challenging, but, with time and direct feedback, open conversations are now the norm. The result is a clear understanding of how each person contributes to the culture they want, an aligned culture that supports purposeful performance.

Apathy is not tolerated, and this comes out clearly in the team's conversations. They regularly build and develop a shared understanding of their guiding principles, clarifying what aligned behaviour is, and, what it is not. Where there are dashes and crosses, shared strategies and actions are developed, focusing on showing desired behaviours, and holding people accountable to change. These plans are reviewed and followed up regularly by the leadership team to enable the ongoing development of a high-performance culture.

Their CEO recently wrote me "Daniel, you helped to reshape the way we lead the business. We have greater trust, transparency and clarity on where we are going, which has given our Board greater confidence in the team, and given me personally a real belief that we can navigate any challenges ahead. It was just the support we needed."

Building an Aligned Organisation of Purposeful Performance is an ongoing process that requires constant work and support. Good leaders build a team, great leaders build leaders. Embedding leadership at every level of your organisation creates an environment of constant evaluation, correction and improvement.

Are you embedding your guiding principles and culture through clarity, empathy and leadership?

- Increase clarity, through sharing stories, asking questions, and frequently repeating guiding principles and behavioural expectations

- Foster empathy, by asking questions as a reflex rather than answering them; ask for disagreement to get new ideas, and find out how people really feel about their work

- Embed leadership, as a capability by recognising and promoting the leadership behaviours of your team, asking for feedback, and never accepting apathy.

Part 5
Managing the Inevitable Tension

Chapter 7

Stop Trying To Get People On Your Bus

Highlights

- Maintaining an aligned culture and strategy means managing the tensions that arise when people aren't committed to the group

- It is vital to address the issues of people who are not working in the same direction as the rest of the team

- People who don't believe in your vision or are not committed to the team must leave the group.

"Leaders set high standards. Refuse to tolerate mediocrity or poor performance."

Brian Tracy

It's an old phrase I've heard many times in my corporate career. Leaders tell their people they need to "get on the bus". Jim Collins coined the metaphor in his excellent book, *Good to Great*, but while he intended it to mean getting the right people in the right seats on a course together, I believe it's frequently misused.

It's used too often in communications, team development and change programs to signal the need for people to accept a new strategy and get on board. The suggestion is that people should either accept the new path (get on the bus) or they'll be left behind (or possibly leave, if they want to), but in my view, that's a poor use of the phrase.

There are several reasons why I think we need a better model. Firstly, let's be very clear, a bus moves whether people are on it or not. People not getting on the bus hardly harm the performance of the bus unless they're the driver. The bus is the same whether it has 30 people crammed in it or just the driver on his own, and if anything, more people on the bus weigh it down slightly, with possibly a marginal negative performance impact.

Secondly, whether people get on willingly, excited about where the bus is going, or under duress, worried about where they're going, the bus route is the same. So, the level of engagement of your people on board doesn't matter, just the number of people on the bus.

But it ignores the two factors that really do matter in any team endeavour:

Do your people believe in the strategic direction of the group? We call this their level of Conviction.

Are your people working cohesively for the success of the group? We call this their level of Commitment.

An alternative metaphor we use is Leading out of the Woods. Imagine a group of people in the middle of the woods, all tied together at the hips by ropes. You need to get to safety, but no one really knows which way safety lies. You are their leader, so you have to choose a direction. This is your Strategy, and your job is to organise and motivate the group to move in that direction as a cohesive unit.

The success of the manoeuvre depends not only on choosing a good strategy, but on ensuring everyone is working together. The further you head in your original direction, the better you'll know if this is the right way or not, which gives you the chance to change direction, but if you can't get people to move you'll never know if your strategy is right or not. You need to move first, and the faster you move, the sooner you'll know if it's the right way or not and adapt. You need your people to have the Conviction to believe in the direction, and the Commitment to move together.

Now, imagine if one of those people thinks your direction is wrong. They think the right way is not in the direction you think - let's say north. Instead, they believe the way to safety is east. If you ignore them, they may try to walk east while the rest of the team walks north, creating tension on the ropes that slows the whole team down. It's likely the people closest to that east-walking person will feel that tension and be frustrated, and some of them may decide to join them, and try to walk east too. This tension, caused by people not believing in your strategic direction, will harm your team performance. This is the Tension of Conviction.

What if one or more of the people in your team don't want to walk, and they just sit down? Unlike our bus metaphor, where they might just flop into a seat and come along for the ride, their sitting down when you're leading people out of the woods creates significant tension on the ropes. Now the rest of your team has to work harder to pull them along through the dirt, so the weight of the people sitting creates a huge drag for everyone else.

The extra effort will naturally be demotivating to many in the group, and resentment builds through having to work extra hard because people are not pulling their weight. Some may even wonder why they should work so hard - maybe they'll just sit down too. This tension, caused by people failing to work as part of the team to steer the group to safety, will affect your team performance significantly. This is the Tension of Commitment, and why the role of a leader and a leadership team are challenging.

To build an aligned organisation, you must ensure your strategy aligns to your guiding principles, that your operating model aligns to your culture, and that these drive purposeful performance. But you also need to actively check that everyone in your organisation understands and believes in your strategy, and will work together effectively as a group. When you adjust one element of an aligned organisation, you need to adjust every other element to remain aligned. Then you have to rebuild the conviction and reinforce commitment. It's a dynamic role, and vital for organisational success.

When you have a Tension of Conviction, what should you do? There are a number of elements to consider: firstly, you need to understand why some of the team see the world differently, to understand their perspectives and to consider their ideas.

If they have good ideas, maybe you can learn from them and integrate them in your strategic planning. Maybe this is a chance for you to explain more, and help them understand your plans better. Sometimes a more intimate conversation leads to greater understanding, and people who didn't believe in your direction become your biggest supporters, the ones who have not taken your strategy for granted, but challenged and tested it thoroughly, and are now ready to work with real conviction. You need passionate people, not passive passengers.

There are also times when you just don't see the world in the same way, and can't possibly agree on certain ideas. This is not to say they are poor performers, bad people or misguided, but there are many successful strategies and sometimes the best thing to do with people who are passionate about a different path is to let them leave. Give them all the support and encouragement you can, but cut the ropes that bind them to the team, and part ways on good terms.

As a leader, it is important to show that you truly support your people, even those who disagree with you. There is no benefit in trying to pull these people into line or force them 'to get on the bus'. Doing this usually only frustrates them, but often people who don't share your beliefs can remain allies if you end the relationship well, and then if your paths cross in the future, it will likely be a positive experience for you both.

When you have a Tension of Commitment - that is people sitting down and being dragged along by your team - this requires a slightly different approach. Once again, you need to understand why they're sitting down, and what is making them feel they don't want to work with the team. If it's because they don't believe they're moving in the right direction, use the

Aligning Culture & Strategy

above strategies. However, if they do generally agree or are ambivalent about the direction and are still dragging their feet, this Tension of Commitment needs you as a leader to act fast.

Lack of commitment to the success of the team is a cancer that spreads quickly and erodes performance. If the team are struggling to keep up, your role as a leader should be to support their skill development, and continue to check whether they can meet expectations.

Some people, no matter how much development you provide, will simply not be able to meet the needs of the group, just as if I were invited to join the Australian 400m relay team - no matter how much training and effort I put in, I would have no chance of contributing to the team's success. If the person can't meet the capability expectations of the group, it's your responsibility as leader to help them find and join another team where they can be successful. Yes, you need to cut them loose, but don't just toss them aside. Do everything you can to help them to find a team or organisation where they can become a valued driver of success.

If it's not a lack of capabilities, but a lack of motivation driving this lack of Commitment, then you may have a freeloader. Using the bus metaphor, this is no big deal - they only take up one seat. But in the woods metaphor, they are a heavy burden for the team, a performance tax paid by everyone, and how you respond to this says a lot about your leadership.

If you turn a blind eye - maybe because you like them or they've performed well in the past – you're signalling to your entire team that sitting down is acceptable, and you are essentially condoning this behaviour. Everyone else in your team will justifiably feel frustrated - why should they have to pull the freeloaders along? It will erode their confidence in your ability to lead, and maybe even encourage them to sit down too. Why work hard if others can slack off? This is how a small group that lacks commitment to the team can bring an organisation to a slow crawl while a few people desperately try to pull them along, and it's both exhausting and demoralising.

Your role as a leader is to set the ideal expectations of the group, and to outline the team's expected behaviours and guiding principles. You don't just set the direction, you also need to set the standards for how you'll work together to get there. So when someone does not meet these expectations, it is your responsibility as a leader to act. You must communicate and reinforce the expectations of the group clearly, and inform people lacking commitment that failure to meet these expectations will mean they can no longer be part of the team. You should support them if they commit to improving their behaviour, but if they are not able to meet expectations you must cut them loose. Again, you can support them as they leave. You can help them to find other teams they may be happier in or which have expectations more aligned with their own, but you can't let your team drag them along.

Whether it is a Tension of Conviction or a Tension of Commitment, these tensions erode the performance of your team, and demotivate those who believe in your direction and are working hard to get there. Addressing these tensions is a critical role of leadership. Too often we try to force people onto the bus, afraid of leaving anyone behind, and thinking that if we have a team of 20, it is important to get all of them on the bus. I disagree.

Leading people out of the woods, I would much rather be part of a smaller team, all focused on working together to a shared set of standards towards a common objective, than fight against my team or, worse, drag bodies through the dirt. Cutting people loose doesn't need to be mean. Sometimes it's exactly what they need to find their path to success. While it might sound a bit harsh, believe me, many of your people who were dragging them will thank you. They might even have a new spring in their step, knowing the injustice of their extra effort has been remedied.

Bumps In The Road

After that initial meeting, we continued to work with the Presta Materials leadership team to develop a detailed strategic plan over the following months, and improve the group's operating rhythm. These sessions identified critical processes to be changed, how to use the guiding principles as well as data and the expertise of team members to make decisions, and how to have more difficult conversations to enable greater understanding within the team.

I was sure things were moving in a more aligned direction, and the leadership team were more open in our sessions so I felt that everyone was committed to the change, but this wasn't so.

Rick and I sat down in the same café as just over a month before. He had called the day before asking for advice on a few things that had developed since the most recent session, and after we had ordered our coffee he handed me a laminated A5 card with a large smile on his face.

At the top, in capital letters, it said Presta GUIDING PRINCIPLES, and below that were four bullet points:

- We look for solutions and follow up until it is done.
- We own mistakes and when things go wrong we make them right.
- We support each other fully and treat loyal people like family.
- We want to make a positive impact on the world.
- We embrace challenging questions and push each other to improve.

"I like the loyalty addition and the clear statement about the impact on the world. I think this is important as a manufacturer. Other than these, you didn't edit them much from the first session." I asked.

"No. We had a meeting about it, and these are close enough. There was something missing about customers and we wanted to show that our people include customers and suppliers. We also agreed, our impact on the world should shape the decisions we make. We spent a lot of time just chatting through situations from the past where these would have come in handy. There were a few words we moved around, and in the end we decided it was better to get on with the job of telling everyone and showing them what we meant by each rather than wordsmithing," Rick replied.

"And how has it been received by the teams?" I asked curiously.

"Generally, great! Sam and Jim have already driven an initiative which both reduces waste and improves our environmental and social impacts. We have had a few issues though. One in particular that I'm keen to get your guidance on." Rick sighed. "Vanessa was the one I was most worried about. I expected her to push back and demand we focus on action, but the good news is that she has basically spearheaded the rollout. I've been so thrilled with her response, and Jim has been working with her to build bridges between their teams, which is great."

"That's fantastic - you had concerns about Jim, and it was pretty clear that Vanessa had reservations before the meeting. Having them on board is a big win. So who are you worried about?" I asked. "I know Sam was a bit cautious after our first session."

"You know, after our first session, I was worried about Sam too. We even met straight away, assuming there would be a lot of pushback, but it just took more time and explanations for Sam to get comfortable with the changes. The problem is Stefan. I'd really thought Stef was on board," Rick said looking disappointed.

"I understand what you mean, but people are complex. I've been in many workshops where the initial reactions are positive, but people struggle to change old behaviours," I replied.

Aligning Culture & Strategy

"Yeah, I feel like Stefan nods in agreement in the sessions, but behind the scenes it's a different story. A few days ago, one of the finance team blew the whistle. They forwarded an email from Stefan through to Sam confidentially where Stef made a joke about the new guiding principles, saying they were the next "Fluff Fad", and basically told his team to ignore them and get on with their work. I wanted to know what you think we should do next." Rick was clearly upset. "Stef has been with us for some time, and he really cleaned up the finance area, which was a mess before."

"What was your first thought when you read the email?" I asked.

"Disappointed, but not totally surprised. Stef sometimes made comments about HR, and had already told me that HR stands for Hardly Relevant. Over a few drinks, he once said that he motivates the whole organisation every fortnight by making sure payroll runs. He's an accountant, and a bloody good one, so I always gave a bit of slack on things like that. But now someone in his team is clearly calling it out as not acceptable, and I feel like it undermines my leadership." Rick sipped his coffee.

"And the work of the whole leadership team," I added. "Rick, the number one team in the organisation is the leadership team. If the people around that table are not aligned, don't trust each other, and don't work as a cohesive unit, it will cause misalignment. This is an issue that needs addressing quickly. We can't have any pirates in the leadership team." I opened my notebook and drew five circles close together on a page.

"Imagine your team is a small group of people trapped in the woods, and you're all tied together at the waist with small ropes," I said, drawing small lines between each circle. "Your job as their leader is to help get them to safety. But you don't know exactly where that is. So, after a discussion with your team, you have to pick a direction and rally the team to walk together, in a coordinated way, in that direction." I drew an arrow towards the top of the page.

"At times, people in the group will think the current direction is wrong. Now, in a high-performing team, there is a discussion about the current direction, and an agreement to either adjust or continue. This is a strategic conversation. But when there's a pirate, they simply pull in a different direction. Walking, let's say, west when the rest of the team is heading north." I drew a small arrow to the left of the circles. "This creates…"

"Tension on the ropes," Rick jumped in, leaning over the page with interest.

"That's right. Now the team is being pulled off the track, and everyone in the team feels the tension. At this point, the leader needs to address this tension." I pointed my pen at the arrow on the left. "Often pirates begin to recruit other people to pull in their direction too, and that can create even more tension and tear a team apart."

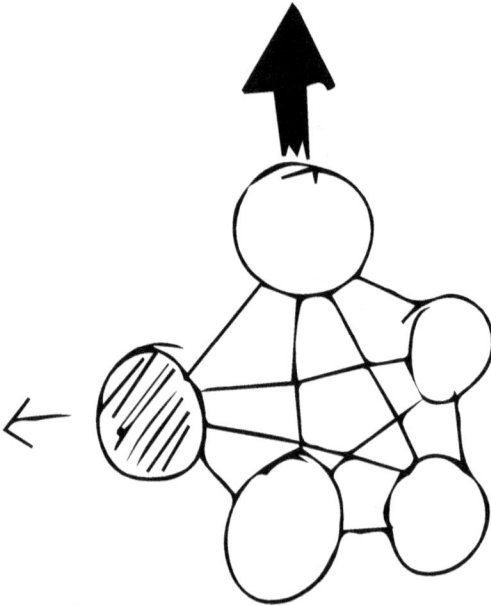

"Like a mutiny," Rick said, pointing to the small arrow. "That email he wrote was like a call to arms against what we are trying to achieve as a team, but what do we do now? I'm nervous that if I say something Stef may just resign, and I don't know what impact that would have on our finance team. Cash flow is pretty tight, and if they drop the ball it could be a massive issue for us."

Rick was clearly facing a common challenge for leaders. How do you balance the need for people to change against the risk that they can't?

"You need to know that doing nothing is not an option, and that when you find a pirate, you need to act, though that doesn't necessarily mean they'll leave or that you have to fire them. Being too reactionary can lead to disruption and chaos for the whole team, and you only have to look at history to find rulers who were too quick to execute any dissenting voices. Remember the story of the Bounty? Captain Bligh's harsh treatment of his men led to the mutiny, but leaders like that tend to have a bad reputation and a short career these days." I paused to sip my coffee.

"Do you really think Stef will come around though? I don't know," Rick interrupted, already considering alternatives.

"I think you need to talk to Stef, and understand why he's pulling in a different direction. There is a possibility that he has valid concerns, and you need to listen with an open mind to see if the direction can be adjusted. But if you find there isn't a need to adjust, then explain what you and the rest of the leadership team are trying to achieve, and see if he really wants to be part of the team. You need to know for sure if he wants to move in this direction, and, if he does, you need to be clear on the changes required," I explained.

Rick decided that he would have a one-on-one conversation with Stefan, and call me afterwards. He arranged a meeting for the next afternoon, and called me not long afterwards. It seemed the discussion hadn't gone as he had hoped.

"He just about exploded," Rick said, still a little shocked. "I told him I was disappointed with the email and his lack of commitment to the leadership team, and that set off a tirade. He said it was all a waste of time, that without him the business would have crumbled, and that what we really need to do is fire Sam so we can bring in someone who gets stuff done."

"That's a shame, but now at least you know what Stefan really thinks about the new direction you and the leadership team are taking. It sounds like your pirate is not too keen on being part of it. What do you think is the next step?" I asked.

"I guess we have to let him go. What else can I do?"

"That may be the case, but I think first you need to clarify a few things. To begin with, how will you handle this in alignment with the guiding principles you're rolling out? If people see Stefan being treated differently, it will show that there are different rules at different times - a sign of misalignment. Next, think about who would be a good replacement. We need to mitigate the risks that his departure, if inevitable, will have on the organisation. Is there anyone in Stefan's team who steps up when he's away?" I asked.

"I always go to Mary Pham when I need something done. She's a safe pair of hands, and knows most of what needs to be done, I think," Rick replied, surprised he hadn't thought of it before.

"Do you think Mary could be a suitable replacement? Your guiding principles mean you'll need everyone in the leadership team to support her."

"Maybe. I think we could manage with her leading the team. We could see how it plays out. But what do I say to Stef?" Rick was worried. He had known Stefan for a long time, and their friendship was important to him. "I don't think one email is justification for firing him. How do I apply our guiding principles here?"

"I would suggest an honest conversation. Remember the second session we had with the leadership team? We made a set of commitments to each other as to how we would behave. Do you think Stef has upheld them?" I was referring to a session where everyone signed their names on a poster of their leadership commitments.

"No, definitely not," Rick replied.

"So, tell him that he hasn't upheld the commitments and guiding principles of the leadership team. Then ask him if he really wants to be a committed member of the team. If he does, then plan what to do together, but if he doesn't, and wants to go in a different direction and leave the business, accept his decision and support him."

"Support him? How?" Rick seemed puzzled by this approach.

"Remember, you're Stef's leader, and you're there to support him. When you are the custodian of your team, you have to support them through the good and the bad, so you should help him to find somewhere that better aligns to the culture he wants to work in. You give an honest reference detailing the great things he's helped you achieve, and, with his permission, you can even put him in touch with companies which need his skills. There's a lot you can and must do if you're going to live the guiding principles on that card. Don't you think so?" I asked, pointing to the laminated card still in front of Rick.

"Take ownership and follow through," Rick said, tapping the card as he picked it up and put it into his bag. "I get it. I need to lead with the guiding principles in mind. This has really helped. I'll give you a call next week after I've seen Stef again."

"Also, Rick, make sure you have plenty of time somewhere you both feel comfortable. When we feel under threat, we tend to react with hostility, and you need to stay calm and objective. You can disagree without being disagreeable. It's okay - we don't always want to head in the same direction, and that doesn't make you right and him wrong, or you good and him bad. You never know when you'll work together again in the future," I said as Rick shook my hand and walked towards his car.

It was another three weeks before I heard from Rick again. His voice on the phone sounded lighter, more energetic than when we had spoken about Stefan. I was eager to hear how the situation had progressed, and what the plan was for the future.

"Stef and I had a really good conversation. We took a few hours over lunch, and had time to really listen to each other. I didn't realise that he had serious ambitions of moving into a CEO or general manager job as his next career step. He's actually applied for a few jobs in larger companies, and, on top of that, he's studying for an MBA at night, and says he's feeling a little burnt out," Rick explained.

"What was your reaction?" I asked.

"I was both surprised he hadn't mentioned it, and embarrassed that I hadn't asked. In the last year, I've been so busy getting on top of things that I lost touch with my team. It was a good reminder to stay close to my people. I now have a weekly check-in meeting with my direct reports. No agenda, often over a coffee, and it's really helped me understand them more," Rick said.

"So, what's the plan for Stef?"

"Stef and I decided it made sense for him to leave, but not straight away. He's working closely with Mary so she can take over from him, and I've asked both of them to come to all the leadership team meetings so we have as smooth a transition as possible," said Rick, more confidently than in our past conversations.

"That sounds like a good plan for Mary and Presta, but what about Stef?" I asked.

"We've agreed to allocate the budget we would have spent on recruiting someone new to a consultant who'll help him find another job, and also reduced his working hours to allow him to study and go to interviews. He's been great ever since, and kept his word," Rick replied.

"What about the broader team? Are you starting to see a change?" I asked.

"Slowly. Every week the leadership team brings up more challenges and problems, but we agree on the measures to take, and are working through them. We're getting better at using the principles to guide us, and everyone is working together much more effectively. In football terms, I feel less like a referee and more like a coach."

"I'm glad to hear it, Rick. There are two things I can guarantee. First, there will never be, should never be, a time when your leadership team meetings have no issues or problems. If you find this happening, there's a good chance you're either not pushing the boundaries enough or people are not raising issues openly. I generally find quiet leadership teams are a danger sign. The second guarantee is that things will keep changing. People may leave, old processes will need updating, new regulations will come in, and new competitors, and new technologies. The world around you will change, and you will need to adapt as a team. You may need to review and refresh your strategy and guiding principles over time too. Always remember, if you change one part, keep looking for the impact, and bring alignment across the organisation."

"Funny you should say that - just last week Vanessa brought up an idea to change order forms for a supplier to integrate with their systems. In the past, she would have made the change and told everyone to get on board.

But her first question was to Jim to find out what impact it might have on the production teams. Next Mary chimed in to discuss ways we could adapt the invoicing process. I asked why we couldn't upgrade all the order forms to create consistency. Now Vanessa and Mary are working together to sketch out how it would work for everyone." Rick chuckled, "You know, this is something we discussed about six months ago and it caused a massive bust up. This is like night and day."

"Now that you have established the guiding principles and started the process of applying them to systems and processes, it is a good time to explore taking this further. Really look to embed them into the way you operate as a business. It would be a matter of building the Presta Materials Playbook. I know you are pressed for time today, but I can come and see you next week to explain further?"

"If it is going to help, I'm all ears. Come by on Friday afternoon, I have some time then," Rick said smiling as he left with a spring in his step.

The Big Question & Actions

Do you have pirates or passengers within your organisation?

- Demonstrate and reiterate clearly and regularly the vision, guiding principles, and standards you expect from your people

- You must manage people who do not share the conviction or commitment of the organisation quickly

- Look after the health of your group by ensuring pirates and passengers do not erode expectations.

Part 6

The Playbook

Chapter 8

Designing the framework for your culture

Highlights

- Embedding guiding principles requires deeper understanding of what they mean and the commitments associated with them
- Using a variety of communication styles allows increased relatability for employees
- Set the tone for your culture with a playbook that becomes a cornerstone of your organisation

"The way a team plays as a whole determines its success. You may have the greatest bunch of individual stars in the world, but if they don't play together, the club won't be worth a dime."

Babe Ruth

A fad is a social phenomenon that gains widespread popularity for a limited period of time. Fads are driven by the desire for people to be part of a trend or to fit in with peers. They are often taken up quickly and fade just as fast once the initial excitement has worn off. One example is the finger spinner craze. These small, handheld devices became extremely popular among schoolchildren in 2017, leading to widespread reports of them being used in classrooms and becoming a distraction from learning. However, by 2018, finger spinners had largely faded from popularity and were no longer seen as widely. This highlights how quickly fads can come and go. While they may seem like they have taken over the world at the time, in reality, they tend to be fleeting phenomena.

Similarly, the roll-out of organisational guiding principles can equally become a momentary fad. The initial excitement and new posters begin to lose their shine and are quickly forgotten. As the examples we have highlighted show, there needs to be more work to embed these new ways of working into the culture of the team. Posters and mouse pads don't stick, we want our people to utilise the guiding principles constantly. We need a more comprehensive way to communicate with the hearts and minds of all people within, and even outside, our organisation.

At this stage in the alignment process, we can increase the impact and longevity of the guiding principles through the creation of an artefact for the organisation. We call this the Guiding Principles Playbook, a document that describes the guiding principles in a variety of ways to create greater clarity and imbue the guiding principles with the unique spirit of the organisation.

The Guiding Principles Playbook is designed to engage multiple areas of the brain to allow your employees to understand the guiding principles from many different perspectives. Some people will find a clear description as enough for them to fully grasp the concepts, however engaging the power of storytelling can deepen understanding and provide more relevant and actionable meaning.

People who crave detail will benefit from examples of key processes and systems that highlight the guiding principles at work. Others in your team will benefit from more abstract modes of communication such as symbols, images and metaphors which engage regions of the right brain more fully. The idea of the playbook is to create an engaging, practical and functional document that can be used constantly for areas such as recruitment, performance management, decision making, process design, dispute resolution and external partnership management.

For each of the guiding principles in the playbook, there are five critical sections we should look to develop as a minimum: Guiding Principle Description, Essential Story, The Metaphor, Definitive Commitments and Key Processes. We also recommend all the guiding principles be formed into a single clear visual model that represents the playbook and helps to increase identity and memorability.

There are an infinite number of variations for the design of the guiding principles playbook and they should be vastly different for every organisation. Unlike the old set of values, the same common words like integrity, trust or respect that everyone else has, your playbook will be unique. It will capture the essence of your organisational culture, it shares insights into who you are and what you stand for. It is like an internal brand design document for your culture. Each section of the playbook provides incredible flexibility in how it is developed but there are some principles that should be considered when designing to maximise effectiveness. Here are some of the features to consider for each section.

Guiding Principle Description

This will be the most familiar to traditional approaches to writing traditional values. Consisting of a headline and a few sentences, the guiding principles description is the basic way of traditionally communicating the value. A good headline is punchy, memorable and acts like a shortcut for the broader description. Avoid long headlines that are hard to share quickly but also avoid single words that are overused and lack any substance.

Great headlines become a shorthand that people use regularly. One of our clients, PDC Tech, had a guiding principle they called No BS. If you are unfamiliar with the term BS, in this case, it stands for bullshit. While the language might be inappropriate for your organisation, it was perfect for theirs. A growing team of electricians working with builders to create amazing store fit-outs across Sydney. No BS is easy to remember and they happily use it in the workplace.

Another headline I like in a registered training organisation is: Assume Good Intent. This simple headline represents such a powerful element of their culture and I've heard people in this organisation say they repeat this to themselves regularly in heated discussions with peers and clients.

Headlines don't have to have rhyme or be an alliteration, but sometimes these are good ways to increase memorability. They don't have to have any set number of words but make sure they aren't too long, save the detail for the sentences that follow the headline. Create the headline as a label people will remember and focus on shaping these to fit with your organisational language.

The description should be a few short sentences that give more information about the headline in a way that expands clarifies the meaning of the headline. Like the headline, it is a chance to be more unique and relatable than a simple dictionary description. Avoid these simple dictionary definitions. This is when companies simply put a word, like integrity, followed by a description that is accurate but horribly uninspiring. Take this example from BHP, one of Australia's largest companies. On their website, one of their values is: Integrity - Doing what is right and doing what we say we will do.

Now contrast this with our client's example.

No BS - We tell the truth. When we make a mistake, we own it, speak up and work together to fix it. We don't hide from problems and we don't try to deceive people. This helps us build trust with everyone we work with.

As you can see, the simple PDC Tech headline represents a significant guiding principlethat helps shape the expectations everyone in the team has for each other. It highlights the need for honesty and some high-level scenarios where it is important. No BS is a powerful shorthand for a guiding principlethat shapes this company to be a trusted service provider to all.

While both BHP and PDC Tech state they integrity as important, there is a stark contrast in the way it is communicated. The uniqueness of no BS brings it to life, it highlights that they have thought about it and documented something that really matters to them. It is their guiding principle and they wear it on their sleeve. BHP's integrity definition could have been written

Aligning Culture & Strategy

by anyone and could just as well be written on the websites of hundreds of other companies.

Google provides a good set of examples of guiding principle descriptions with what they call their - Ten things we know to be true. Here are two examples from Google, both showing a simple headline that is easy to remember and a description that provides more information on the guiding principles. You can find all ten at about.google/philosophy.

1. Focus on the user and all else will follow.

Since the beginning, we've focused on providing the best user experience possible. Whether we're designing a new Internet browser or a new tweak to the look of the homepage, we take great care to ensure that they will ultimately serve you, rather than our own internal goal or bottom line. Our homepage interface is clear and simple, and pages load instantly. Placement in search results is never sold to anyone, and advertising is not only clearly marked as such, it offers relevant content and is not distracting. And when we build new tools and applications, we believe they should work so well you don't have to consider how they might have been designed differently.

2. You can be serious without a suit.

Our founders built Google around the idea that work should be challenging, and that the challenge should be fun. We believe that great, creative things are more likely to happen with the right company culture—and that doesn't just mean lava lamps and rubber balls. There is an emphasis on team achievements and pride in individual accomplishments that contribute to our overall success. We put great stock in our employees—energetic, passionate people from diverse backgrounds with creative approaches to work, play and life. Our atmosphere may be casual, but as new ideas emerge in a café line, at a team meeting or at the gym, they are traded, tested and put into practice with dizzying speed—and they may be the launch pad for a new project destined for worldwide use.

Creating a good headline and guiding principle description can take time. Don't feel the need to rush to completion or make it too fancy. They can always be adjusted, especially once you develop some of the other sections.

Essential Story

The next section for the playbook is your essential story. This is ideally a real example of where this guiding principle was used to make a decision or resolve a challenge in a way that typifies how it should be used.

Sharing stories is one of the most ancient ways humans have passed on wisdom. For thousands of years we sat around the campfire and shared tales and myths that conveyed critical information.

After the Boxing Day Tsunami, there were grave fears held for many of the indigenous communities living on the remote islands in the Andaman sea. Closest to the epicentre of the earthquake that triggered the tsunami, these small islands were directly in the firing line of the huge waves that would go on to take the lives of over 250,000 people. Having seen the devastation in much more developed places across Indonesia and Thailand, anthropologists feared for these ancient and reclusive tribes.

To their surprise, there were almost no casualties in these tiny, isolated communities. When the earthquake was felt by the islanders, most of them knew to watch the water. Stories had been passed down through the generations of tsunamis. Not in any scientific sense, many tell of times when the ocean and the forest fight. After the earth shakes, the land will try to take ground from the ocean. Then the ocean will fight back and water will rush into the forest with great fury. After the earthquake, the people of these islands saw the tide recede and knew what to do.

In many places, the receding water was ignored or even met with curiosity. Sad images showed tourists walking out across the sandy plains created by the approaching wall of water, not realising the imminent danger they were in. However, the ancient stories of the battles between land and sea sent the inhabitants of these small islands immediately running into the mountains to safety. While humans have passed on fantastic tales for thousands of years, in organisations, the most effective essential stories are real experiences. True stories that are easy to understand, relatable to your people and obvious in the way the guiding principles were demonstrated are the most effective.

Aligning Culture & Strategy

Essential stories can capture the decisions or actions of people from any level or department in the organisation, it doesn't need to be something the CEO. In large organisations, a variety of stories from different levels and departments can help your people relate more easily. If they are stories people see as a situation they would never be faced with or a decision they don't think they would be empowered to make, the stories won't as easily become an essential part of the organisational culture.

Simplicity can also be an important aspect of great essential stories. They should not only be written down but also be shared by your people verbally. Richard Branson's famous origin story of starting Virgin Airlines is an example of just how their simplicity can spread across industries. In the early 80's, Branson found himself stuck in Puerto Rico desperate to get back to his girlfriend on the British Virgin Islands. When the American Airlines flight was cancelled, Branson was livid.

Already a successful entrepreneur, Branson did what people at Virgin do. He looked for a solution. He used his credit card to charter a plane then marched through the airport with a chalkboard that said "Virgin Airlines one-way: $39 to the Virgin Islands". The plane filled and the very next day, Branson called Boeing: "I'm thinking of starting an airline called Virgin. Do you have any secondhand 747s for sale?"

The Virgin Airlines origin story, like the Zappo's pizza story from Chapter 5, can become powerful beacons for any organisation. They can give guidance and even permission to employees, align with expectations of customers and reinforce brand values to the external market. Like all stories throughout history, they may be told differently over time, sometimes gaining a few parts or skimping on some details. The essence though is in the guiding principles they reinforce.

The Metaphor

A further way of communicating the meaning of guiding principles is to use a Metaphor. By metaphor, we will refer to a broader category of concepts that may include similies, symbols, images and analogies that help us share complex and nuanced meaning in simpler to remember ways that are easier to share than wordier definitions.

Metaphors are powerful, bite-sized ways of sharing concepts in simplified ways that contextualise meaning. These abstract models can describe organisational guiding principles in ways that are similar to our best understanding of how our brains make meaning. Through identifying patterns and analogical reasoning, we are able to navigate situations and solve problems that we have never faced before.

Let's take recruitment as an example. The process of attracting, interviewing and securing new employees into an organisation. At this level, it is a simple process flow, but anyone who has been through the recruitment process knows that they are anything but straightforward. Depending on the particular role, company brand, team cohesion, business performance, role location and the socio-economic conditions, the recruitment process can vary greatly.

If I told you my current recruitment process was like finding a needle in a haystack, I'd likely not need to share any data for you to understand the challenges more easily. You wouldn't know exactly what is going on, but of all the possible recruitment experiences possible, you instantly have a better understanding of my current experience. Alternatively, if I said it was like shooting fish in a barrel or pulling teeth, you will form different ideas of the experience. Recruitment is never like any of these things, please don't shoot fish in barrels, but our brains understand the abstract meanings of te metaphors and use this to align with a cluster of the vast number of recruitment scenarios.

Metaphors help create a deeper, subconscious understanding through abstract associations, unconstrained by specific facts, data or processes. This lack of constraint enables greater transference of meaning to a larger variety of situations. If I said developing a new product was like a needle in a haystack, shooting fish in a barrel or pulling teeth, the same set of

Aligning Culture & Strategy

associations as with recruitment can be made even though these processes are very different.

Building a metaphor or image that represents your guiding principles can become a pivotal way of transferring the essence of the meaning transferrable across the vast spans of your organisation. When you start looking for metaphors, they are actually everywhere in organisations. From statements like "our business is anchored in shared guiding principles" to "the transformational journey of technology", metaphors are a very natural way to communicate and share ideas.

Atlassian has grown from two young Australian founders with a dream and a ten thousand dollar credit card to $34 billion dollar software giant. One of their core values is to 'Build with heart and balance'. On its own, this is a broad and concept so to bring this to life they use a simple metaphor: "Measure twice, cut once". While heart and balance can mean a variety of things, this old carpentry metaphor tells their people to consider what they are doing carefully and not to let their passion or urgency create unneccisary challenges.

Salesforce describe their values as their "guiding compass" with a cartoon image of someone scaling a mountain holding a compass accompanied by a larger image of a compass surrounded by their values of Trust, Customer Success, Sustainability, Innovation and Equality. They want people to strive to climb but make sure they are considering these values with each step.

Choosing your metaphor can be difficult. Often the more we think logically we become too literal and our ideas become less creative or abstract. A useful way to develop metaphors is to start with an array of various images, then ask people to select those that they feel represent the meaning of the value. This allows the subconscious and emotional associations to be identified more readily.

For example, when discussing with a client a guiding principle they had formed: "Supporting our people" we showed them images of an ambulance, a sports coach and training wheels on a bike. These three images all showed elements of support, but the team quickly identified the ambulance as the closest. "We are there for each other when times get tough or when someone is in trouble," said one of the executive team.

The ambulance wasn't quite right, but it helped us land on a metaphor inspired by the US Army Rangers. The Ranger Creed which states: "Never shall I fail my comrades. I will never leave a fallen comrade to fall into the hands of the enemy." This helped them land on the metaphorical representation of this guiding principle as two soldiers walking arm in arm, a powerful guiding principle that resonates through the organisations when they face inevitable challenges. I've witnessed people in the leadership team put their arm around each other to show their support, an act which holds greater significance due to this metaphor.

Definitive Commitments

Sir Ralph Norris, the former CEO of Commonwealth Bank, used to speak to employees often about his 'Sundown' and 'TOFU' rules. The Sundown rule stated that if someone contacted you during the day via email or voice message, you would get back to them by sundown. Even if it was only to say that you would contact them again the next day, at least acknowledge their message for you. This was a simple concept that was shared often by various people across the group and represented the respect we should show each other in acknoweldging each other in a timely manner.

TOFU stood for take ownership, follow up. This meant that is you come across an problem, encounter a dispute or even contacted by someone by mistake, don't ignore it. Instead, take ownership to resolve the situation. Take accountability to see it through and follow up to make sure it has been fixed. This was a call to action for everyone to commit to fixing the issues that arise in the organisation.

These types of calls to action are what we refer to as Commitments. Statements that clearly direct behaviour in line with the guiding principles of the organisation. These commitments are more clear and direct instructions for action than the abstract metaphors and engaging stories. They highlight what you and your people should be doing to align to the guiding principles. This sounds obvious but is often where guiding principles fail to get traction.

Australia's largest telecommunications company, Telstra, have been on a long and challenging journey to turn around their notoriously poor reputation in customer service. One way they are addressing this is

Aligning Culture & Strategy

through their Customer Service Commitments. Below are a number of the statements Telstra make:

- We are committed to being available 24x7 for you to report any faults or service difficulties.

- We are committed to maintaining a Sales Watch Hotline, where you can report instances of unethical sales behaviour you experience.

- We are committed to presenting your telephone bill in a form that suits your needs, with options including online, paper, large print and Braille.

- We are committed to dealing with your concerns or complaints promptly, fairly, completely and courteously informing you of how we propose to act, how long it should take and what the results are.

These statements are designed to both set expectations with their customers, and, to instruct and guide their employees. Telstra has said they are focused on customers for many years, sadly their consumer rating on sites like trustpilot.com and customerservicescoreboard.com has remained very low. Once expectations have been broken and confidence is low, it is a very long road to recovery. Changing the guiding principles won't help build your reputation, it will be the millions of interactions between Telstra's people with their customers that align to these commitments that will slowly reshape their reputation over time.

Commitments are also a useful way to test our guiding principles. Early in my work on building organisational guiding principles, I was working with a CEO who told me he wanted to "put our people first" as one of their guiding principles. This is a noble principle and I initially thought I was clear on his intent. I then asked him a question:

"Imagine you have a meeting booked with one of your direct reports and, just as you are about to go to the meeting, your phone rings and it is a client who wants a conversation. What would you do?" He looked at me and said, "I guess it depends how big a client it was".

This was a critical moment. Guiding principles naturally create behavioural expectations. Creating and sharing a set of guiding principles requires everyone, but particularly leaders, to make a commitment to uphold these guiding principles. Otherwise they will become just empty ideals that do not shape the culture. One of the best ways to do this is to write sentences that start with the words: I will always.... and I will never...

Here are some illustrative examples of Definitive Commitments that could be developed for guiding principles.

Guiding Principles	Definitive Commitment
Open transperency	We will never hold back information that is useful to others We will always be proactive in helping people get the information they need
Defend the vulnerable	We will always stand up for people in need no matter the cost We will never leave a vulnerable person in a time of need
Customers success is paramount	We will never put the profit of the business ahead of the success of a customer We will always see a customer through to a successful outcome
Don't take success for granted	We will always review our wins to understand learn how we can improve We will never stop challenging ourselves and each other to improve
Build a positive team	We will never speak poorly of our team members We will always look for the best in our peers and celebrate their talents
Challenge the status quo	We will always look for new ways to do what we do today We will never defend the way we do something today at the cost of exploring a new way

Aligning Culture & Strategy

Yes, these commitments can feel uncomfortable at first. They are constrictive and provide limited wiggle room. Worries will begin to emerge as people imagine scenarios where they might struggle to uphold them. These exceptions worry people and they want to change them to include loopholes. Clients often ask if they can add words like 'mostly, try or except when'. They are worried that by creating commitments with the words always and never that they are setting themselves up for inevitable failure.

The problem is, for your guiding principles to be truly meaningful tools that guide and shape your culture, they need to be definitive. They need to be hard to maintain. When we create loopholes, we erode conviction. At a conference once I was asked by an audience member if we have the right to judge each other. My response to her was simple, whether we have the right to or not, everyone judges other people all the time. It is a natural and instinctive act we subconsciously perform all the time. We are always judging others and others are judging us. We can't control if others are judging us, we can only control our actions.

When our customers, employees, peers and stakeholders judge us, it is not on how clever the words are that we say are our guiding principles, they judge us on the alignment between the expectations they have, which may be shaped by our stated guiding principles, and our actions. The thing we lose when we fail to uphold our guiding principles and commitments through our actions is one of the most precious commodities: Trust.

Trust is precious and every time we say we stand for a principle and then behave in a way that contradicts this, we break trust with people. Creating loopholes in commitments simply highlights a lack of conviction for them. Building a set of definitive commitments helps to ground guiding principles into behaviours that everyone can hold each other accountable to. These should be a small set of statements for each guiding principle that bring to life the commitment and conviction you have to that value.

Key Processes

The most tangible way to communicate and reinforce guiding principles is through the key processes and policies that have been developed to ensure these guiding principles are upheld systematically. There are few things more frustrating to employees and customers than processes and policies that undermine the guiding principles that they are told to uphold. Unfortunately, we see this all too often in modern organisations. As we discussed in Chapter 7, call centres tell their workers to care about customers via posters on the walls only to develop measurement dashboards and remuneration processes that encourage efficiency over customer service.

In committing to your guiding principles, there should be clear trade-offs that are made and codified into systems, processes and policies throughout the organisation. By highlighting these key processes in the Playbook, it creates a set of specific examples of where decisions have been made to ensure these principles guide action.

At luxury hotel chain Ritz-Carlton, every employee at any level is empowered to spend up to $2,000 to solve a customer issue without needing any permission from management. Their motto is: "We are Ladies and Gentlemen serving Ladies and Gentlemen." The Ritz-Carlton want to make sure their customers are looked after, not that they will need to speak to a manager or wait for someone to get sign off from the head office. The ladies and gentlemen who work for the Ritz-Carlton know, if there is a problem, they have the authority to spend up to $2,000 to solve it on the spot.

Examples of this rule in action abound. A facilities manager who was busy changing a light bulb was asked by a guest how long it would take to get to the airport as they were in a hurry. The facilities manager stopped what he was doing and took them to the airport personally. A guest complained about the noise of children from a nearby room who were playing hockey in the hallway. A member of staff went to the boys room and suggested they could use the empty ballroom to play hockey. They also gathered up a few other staff members and joined the boys in a game of hockey.

These policies and processes are only valueable if they are used. Too many companies make promises with a series of footnotes and loopholes that actually mean they are largely useless. Insurance companies who run great marketing campaigns claiming they are there to help but in the fineprint describe all the reasons they won't help in your specific situation. Jewellry stores who claim to be having a big sale and price an item as familybeing reduced from $500 to $300 when they have never stocked the product at the higher price. And of course the real estate agents who claim

Pizza chain Domino's have a 20 minute delivery guarantee. If your pizza is not delivered within 20 minutes of you completing your order, they will give you a voucher for a free pizza. They do state with this guarantee that it only applies where travel time will mean it is safe to deliver in this amount of time, but the guarantee tells customers and employees that speed is a core principle of Domino's. A potentially frustrating but important footnote in this case.

Patagonia go further in embedding their guiding principles. The outdoor-apparel company doesn't just try to greenwash their brand with lofty statements about reducing their carbon footprint. They see themselves as activists for the environment and encourage their employees to be also. Patagonia offer their people civil disobedience training to learn how to protest safely and effectively. They take this even one step further. If you have completed the training and are arrested while protesting for a cause, the company will pay for your bail. Their founder and CEO, Yvon Chouinard said in and interview: "We don't have a just society, and that's when you need civil disobedience, absolutely."

Patagonia also believe in being a family company. In their corporate head office, they have an on-site childcare facility for staff. Not only do their children get looked after but parents are also envcouraged to interact with their children, share lunch and play during the day. This isn't a knee jerk reaction to some HR trend either, they have has this in place since the 1980's. If you are going to tell people you are a family business, then build facilities that bring this to life. Nothing reinforces a family business better than seeing your colleagues playing in a sandpit with their children.

In reality, until the guiding principles you describe at the beginning of your Playbook start to materialise as systems, processes and policies that code them into the organisation, they can always be seen as just empty words. The Key Processes should be a collection of the ways in which the organisation has begun the codification of guiding principles, but not the end of this process. In the most value-led organisations, they are always looking at what they do today and challenging as to whether this is really aligned to the guiding principles or not. As we discussed in chapter 7, it is easy for guiding principles and processes to part ways and create a culture you didn't intend.

The Presta Playbook

Renée Samson was excited. It was a sunny Monday morning and walked into the head office of Presta Materials to start her new role as Payroll Manager. It was a big step. After completing her business degree and working in the payroll department of a large corporation for a few years, Renée felt this was her first big chance to make an impact. She had been searching for a smaller organisation and when the role at Presta came up, she jumped at the opportunity.

"Welcome Renée, so great to see you again! Flat white with one sugar, right?" said Mary Pham holding out a white keep-cup with 'RENEE' on the side. Mary had been promoted to the role of Presta's Finaicial Officer over a year ago now and this was one of her first big recruitments into the team.

"Wow, thanks!" said Renée, accepting the coffee.

"How was your trip in? Is the commute okay?" asked Mary.

"It was different. I would usually get the train from home towards the city but it was a nice change heading out here. Far less crowded," replied Renée not mentioning that it took her around 45 minutes longer than her previous commute.

"I know it is probably a bit longer than your old trip into the city too," said Mary, "so, let's talk about what time you should leave today so you don't feel unsafe making a new trip in the dark."

Mary walked with Renée to the offices of each of the senior leaders at Presta. Each time, Renée was surprised to see them greet her so warmly.

Rick Hampton was on a phone call, but when he saw Mary and Renée walk past promptly told the person to hold for a second while he walked out to greet them.

"Welcome to the Presta family Renée, we are so excited to have you join us." Rick said, a smile spread across his face. "Has Mary given you the PVP yet?"

"Not yet, but I have one right here," Mary said, tapping a glossy booklet in her hand.

"Great. Please ask myself or any of the team if you have any questions about the PVP. My copy is never far from reach," said Rick pointing a copy of the glossy booklet on his desk.

"Sorry, what is the PGP?" Renée asked a little sheepishly.

"Sorry, Rick likes to use acronyms at times. It is the Presta Guidiung Principles Playbook. I mentioned in the interview that we have a way of doing things here at Presta. The playbook is the guide on how that all works," Mary chimed in, again tapping the booklet with her hand.

"Sorry, I do love a three letter acronym. The playbook is like our bible for how we work here at Presta. We've put a lot of work into developing it and, while it is pretty good, we are always open to ideas on how we can improve it. I'd love to grab a coffee with you in a week or two and hear any thoughts you have about it," said Rick.

"Okay, I will," replied Renée, surprised Rick would be interested in her opinions.

Lastly, they walked past the offices of Sam Stevenson, Presta's Head of People, Culture & Risk. As they entered the small office, Sam picked up a keep cup off the table covered in a rainbow pattern.

"Welcome, I can see you got your keep cup? We brought these in to reduce the number of paper cups we used and to stop there being a dozen or more dirty mugs in the sink. It also increases the ability for everyone to show a bit more of themselves at work. You can order a customised wrap to go around these cups to show a bit more of who you are," said Sam.

Aligning Culture & Strategy

"Mine has a image of my son and I on holidays recently in New Zealand," said Mary. "Once you settle in, I can give you the website link to design your own, they only take a few days to arrive."

"Cool, my Mum will be happy. She always gets annoyed when the acute accent is left off the second e," Renée said a little sheepishly. "I mean it is no big deal, it happens all the time."

"Your mother is right, it shouldn't be left off. Wait there a second," said Mary as she ran back towards her office in a hurry.

"Umm... where is she going?" asked Renée.

"To make it right would be my guess," answered Sam with a broad smile.

Mary appeared from her office briskly walking back down the hallway with a marker pen in her hand. She reached a hand out toward Renée.

"Can I have your cup for a second?" Mary asked. Renée obliged, carefully handing her the still warm coffee. Mary carefully turned the cup in her hand held up towards her face, used her teeth to pull the lid off the marker pen and drew a small accent to make it an é.

"That's better. So sorry for getting that wrong Renée, that was my fault for not checking. I'll be sure to get it right from now on," Mary apologised returning the lid on her marker.

"You didn't have to do that Mary, it's fine," Renée said.

"As you'll find out in the PVP, at Presta Materials, we own mistakes when things are wrong, and do what it takes to make them right. It is one of our guiding principles. To be honest, I was just about to grab a marker myself," said Sam with a broad smile.

"This PVP sounds important, I better study it closely," said Renée matching Sam's smile.

"Don't worry, once you have read through it, you will see the PVP everywhere. We use it in planning, strategy, sales and even in recruitment. Remember when I told you we used a spreadsheet for exception management? You immediately asked why we used a spreadsheet, offered a few other ways you'd seen companies manage exceptions differently and even sent me a link to an article on the topic. That was what really attracted us to you as the new Payroll Manager," said Mary.

"Oh right, is the exceptions management was that big a problem?" asked Renée.

"No, not at all. In fact, since your email we've already implemented a pilot program to test one of the solutions and are hoping you will see the full integration if the pilot is successful," Mary explained. "You were the only candidate who challenged the way we did things when I mentioned the spreadsheet. Not only did you ask why we use a spreadsheet, but you proactively suggested multiple solutions to fix it."

Mary opened the playbook in her hand to a page titled 'We look for solutions and follow up until it is done.' The page had a large picture of a jigsaw puzzle on the lefthand side and a number of different boxes with text.

"That's one of the biggest things we look for in the interview process here Renée," said Sam. "We want to see an alignment between the candidate and our guiding principles here at Presta. After that interview, Mary was really confident you were the right person."

"And once we checked out the information you sent, the team got excited enough to set up a pilot," said Mary.

"Wow, at my last company people would have complained about having to do more work. They always did things the same as they had always done it. I think I'm going to like it around here," Renée said while looking at the playbook and smiling. "They sure could have used this playbook!"

Mary and Renée then spent the next hour meeting other people in the team. Mary showed Renée to her allocated desk and introduced her to Tammy who managed all the IT set up.

"Once Tammy has got you set up, I'd suggest spending the rest of the day reading through the PVP," said Mary, leaving the book on her desk. "Once you have read through, we can catch up again so I can answer any questions you might have."

Aligning Culture & Strategy

"Okay, thanks Mary," replied Renée before switching her attention back to the files Tammy was showing her on her computer. Once Tammy left, Renée opened up her copy of the Presta Guiding Principles Playbook and started to read through.

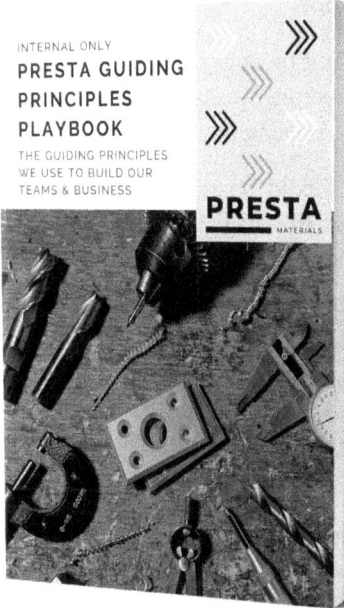

INTERNAL ONLY
PRESTA GUIDING PRINCIPLES PLAYBOOK
THE GUIDING PRINCIPLES WE USE TO BUILD OUR TEAMS & BUSINESS

PRESTA MATERIALS

Renée was sitting at her desk, staring at the playbook. This wasn't like anything she had ever seen at her last job. She was surprised, excited and a little scared all at the same time. Renée walked over and poked her head through the doorway of Mary's office. She saw Mary was in conversation with someone. She recognised her from her research on Presta as Vanessa Matthews, Head of Customers and Sales. Vanessa was an imposing figure with a striking red pant suit and powerful looking figure that made her seem larger than life. Renée had read on LinkedIn that Vanessa was a ruthless manager at her former company and had made a mental note to stay clear of her.

"Renée, come in," said Vanessa in a loud and confident voice. "It's nice to meet you, I'm Vanessa, I'm responsible for customers and sales here at Presta. I hear you are the new Payroll Manager, I best be extra kind to you, right? Welcome to the community, Mary is thrilled to have you join us here. How can we help?"

"Oh it's nothing important, I can come back," replied Renée, hoping to avoid Vanessa at least on day one.

"Actually Renée, you might be able to help. Vanessa and I are looking at a few different ways to structure rebates to a set of customers for one of our product lines," said Mary, walking to a small whiteboard in her office.

"See, Mary thinks we should share the rebates equally across all the customers who purchase the Mag-3Q's and I think we should make it at least volume scaled to incentivise increased volumes," said Vanessa in a relaxed tone.

Mary drew a line down the middle of the board writing headings on each side of it: Equal and Scaled.

"Umm... I'm not sure," replied Renée uneasily.

"Of course you are not sure Renée, how could you be? This is your first day. We don't want you to give us a perfect answer, but we want to know what you think. We already know what we think and it is getting us stuck," said Vanessa with a warm smile.

"Well, I guess if you spread it equally it is fair, but what if some of the customers are more loyal to us than others? We could support them more with greater rebates?" Renée said, pointing to the Equal side of the board. "Equally, larger volumes might mean larger revenue for us, but what if customers order more for the rebates and undervalue the products. Could that create unnecessary waste?"

Vanessa and Mary looked at each other and smiled.

"Now that is more like it," said Vanessa, grabbing a whiteboard marker and putting bullet points on both sides to reflect Renée's comments. For the next half-hour, they stood around the whiteboard discussing, debating and challenging the different ways the rebate could be done.

As they were leaving, Vanessa turned to Renée and said, "I have a feeling you will fit in perfectly here Renée."

So what next?

This book was designed as a guide to developing and leading an Aligned Organisation. It has focused on:

- Bringing a level of alignment and harmony to the ways tangible and intangible elements of your organisation come together to be greater than the sum of their parts

- How to avoid the tensions that pull too many teams apart, and how to empower your people to lead from within.

- Providing some tools and insights to help you implement the Aligned Organisational Model: the two elements (Tangible and Intangible) and three phases (Planning, Execution and Outcome).

- Creating a Playbook to ensure the guiding Principles are captured, communicated and embedded into the hearts and minds of your people and the actions they take each day.

One more challenge you may face is that you don't always see what is right in front of you. If you're wearing clothes at the moment, there's a good chance you haven't noticed how they feel on your skin until now, when I brought it to your attention. As we mentioned earlier, our brains ignore a lot of incoming information. They have to for us to survive.

This is why great employees sometimes leave, frustrated by problems they think the boss is ignoring. Sometimes that boss (perhaps you) just doesn't see the problems at all. These blind spots are deadly, and there's a good chance, if you're human, you have some right now.

Aligning Culture & Strategy

While curiosity is a great way to uncover and overcome them, there is another way. Get a fresh set of eyes. Bringing in new people, new perspectives and fresh thinking is vital to uncovering blind spots and building a better future.

External consultants sometimes have a bad reputation for taking your watch and telling you the time - but then sometimes you don't even realise you're wearing a watch!

At Empathic Consulting, we ask questions that our clients may not have thought of, because we see the world differently. Not better or worse, but from another perspective, and it is this new perspective that shines a light on blind spots, and allows significant breakthroughs.

If you need help in developing an aligned organisation, we'd love to support your journey.

PRESTA GUIDING PRINCIPLES PLAYBOOK

THE GUIDING PRINCIPLES WE USE TO BUILD OUR TEAMS & BUSINESS

PRESTA
MATERIALS

WHAT YOU WILL FIND IN THIS PLAYBOOK

Table of contents

About the Presta guiding principles Playbook.................2

The Guiding Principles
- We look for solutions and follow up until
  it is done... 3

- We own mistakes when things go wrong, and make them
  right... 5

- We support each other fully and treat loyal people like
  family.. 7

- We want to make a positive impact on
  the world.. 9

- We embrace challenging questions and push each other to
  improve.. 11

What next?..13

ABOUT PRESTA MATERIALS

Presta Materials was founded in 1973 in Mascot, Sydney originally creating machinery for garment manufacturing. Today, Presta materials is a -based company that provides high-quality products and services to a variety of clients across Australia. We are committed to being a professional and fun company to work with, and our guiding principles everything we do.

Our products are made with the highest quality materials and craftsmanship, and our team is dedicated to providing outstanding customer service. We believe that by providing great products and services, we can make a positive difference in the lives of our clients and the world. We are proud to be a part of the Presta family and strive to always improve for ourselves, our clients and our community,

THE PRESTA PLAYBOOK

At Presta Materials, we believe that our success comes from living our guiding principles and behaving in ways that reflect our guiding principles. We call this the Presta Playbook.

The objective of the Presta Playbook is to ensure that everyone in our organisation is clear on our guiding principles, what we stand for and what we expect of each other as members of the Presta family.

By living our guiding principles, we create a culture of performance that goes beyond simply meeting goals or hitting targets. Our guiding principles inspire us to be our best selves, work together as a team and make a positive impact on our customers, our communities and the world around us.

We are proud of the Presta Playbook and the role it plays in helping us achieve our mission. While it is good today, it will never be perfect. It is an expectation of all employees to read, understand and live the guiding principles enclosed in this playbook. Also, we expect you to challenge what is here and suggest any changes we could make that would support our mission.

Rick Hampton
Managing Director
Presta Materials

WE LOOK FOR SOLUTIONS & FOLLOW UP UNTIL IT IS DONE.

Search for the pieces until the puzzle is complete

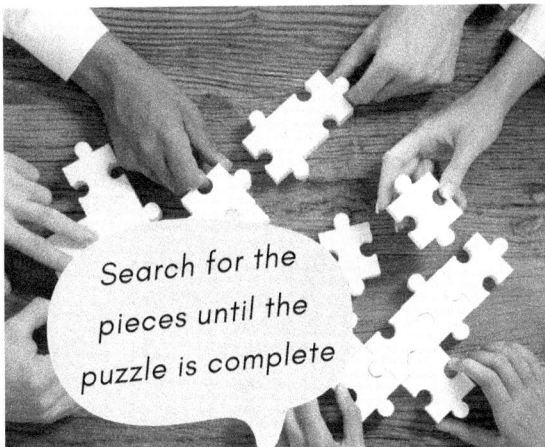

Value Description

We will always face challenges, as will our peers, customers and suppliers. It's how we deal with these challenges that define us as an organisation. At our core, we are problem solvers. We don't give up when things get tough - we work hard, together, to find a way to overcome the obstacles in our path. Our tenacity is what sets us apart from competitors.

We don't just want things to work - we are determined to make sure they are the right solutions, no matter what it takes. This is who we are, and this is what we stand for. When people work with us, they can rest assured knowing that we won't give up on them. We see it through to a successful end. That's our commitment to each other, and it's something that we take very seriously.

Definitive Commitments

- We will always see problems as opportunities to explore new ways of doing things
- We will never leave a job half complete, what we start we finish
- We do things properly or we don't do them at all
- We always make sure the job is complete, close enough is not good enough

We look for solutions & follow up until it is done.

Essential Story

Martin and Jim were at a client's worksite when one of the machines broke down. The failure was from a number of parts that were worn out and had not been replaced as scheduled. Martin was able to source most of the pieces from our local warehouse, but two vital parts were not in stock.

Jim called ten different suppliers before locating the parts through a competitor. He was able to get the parts couriered within two hours and they worked on-site for another three hours, but they finally got the machine up and running again. Thanks to Jim's perseverance, they managed to get the client production up again.

Martin thought there was more they could do. Over the next week, he built them an improved maintenance schedule that included parts supplied by Presta and two competitors. He even helped them develop a simple process for ordering that saves the client delivery costs and reduces the risk of failures in the future.

Key Processes - ways we have embedded the guiding principles into our routine

- **Flex to Complete Policy -** When deadlines will impact our health or the quality of our work, everyone has the discretion to initiate a discussion to review the scope and timelines. If a Flex to Complete conversation is dismissed, this should be immediately escalated to a senior leader.

- **Bright Spark meetings** - These 45 min meetings can be called by anyone with a maximum of 6 attendees. Invitations are sent with the title 'Bright Spark' and a 100-word or less explanation of the problem. Invitees are asked to help find solutions to the specific problem. If you are invited and available, you should attend and support the solution exploration process.

- **Bright Spark Report-back** - To ensure we follow up, every Bright Spark meeting should have an update email sent to all attendees no later than 2 weeks after the meeting to share learnings and feedback from the solution session.

GUIDING PRINCIPLE 2

A mistake is a chance to make it better than before

WE OWN MISTAKES & WHEN THINGS GO WRONG WE MAKE THEM RIGHT.

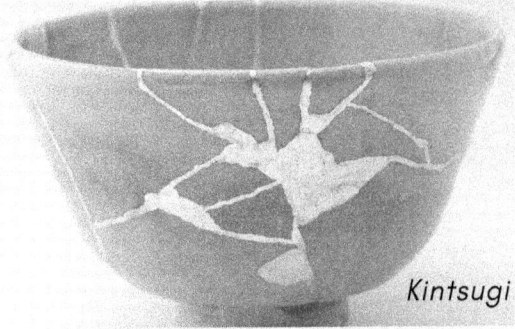

Kintsugi

Value Description

At some point, we all make mistakes. We drop a glass and it shatters. We drop food and stain our clothes. We misplace an important file and can't find it when we need it. While these mishaps can be frustrating, they also give us an opportunity to learn and grow. In Japanese culture, there is a concept called kintsugi, which means "golden joinery." This philosophy teaches us that breakage is not something to be hidden or ashamed of, but rather an opportunity. We don't try to hide our mistakes.

At Presta Materials, we believe that every mistake has the potential to make us better. Mistakes are not shameful, they are a natural side-effect of trying our best in a busy and chaotic world. The focus is always on owning and acknowledging our mistakes, supporting others when they make mistakes, finding ways to remedy any damage caused and ensuring we all learn from the experience.

Definitive Commitments

- We will never hide out mistakes or look to blame others for our errors
- We will always assume our peer's mistakes weren't intentional
- We will always debrief with our peers about mistakes to improve learning
- We will never hold mistakes against someone who is honest about them

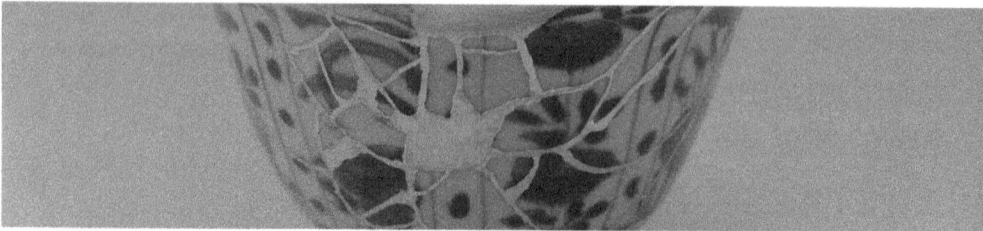

We own mistakes & when things go wrong we make them right.

Essential Story

Mary had always been conscientious and detail-oriented in her work. So when she made a simple error that caused the company to underpay some of our employees, she was devastated. The mistake was discovered after a few months meaning there was a lot of work to reconcile the underpayments.

Mary immediately told everyone in the company about the issue and apologised, explaining that it was a mistake she had personally made. She worked tirelessly to identify every underpayment, checked everyone had been paid correctly and compensated impacted employees. She also implemented a new control system that checks each payment to reduce future errors.

She also gave each person a handwritten card apologising for the mistake and expressing her gratitude for their hard work. By taking ownership of the problem and fixing it, Mary enhanced the trust of the finance team in the eyes of her colleagues and demonstrated her dedication to fixing errors.

Key Processes - ways we have embedded the guiding principles into our routine

- **The Fixed It Awards -** Each quarter, 5 people who have found new ways of improving or made an error and fixed it successfully are invited to present a short case study of their situation to the entire organisation at a celebration event. We then all vote for the best example and the winner is issued with a Fixed It trophy and prize.

- **Risk Review Meeting** - After any mistake within a team, the Manager is to call an all-team meeting to review the mistake and perform a risk management review to identify adjacent risks associated with the mistake to improve our risk framework.

- **Big Mistakes Wall** - All large errors are documented in a one-page case study, laminated and shared on the Big Mistakes Wall. Employees are encouraged to regularly review the wall, particularly when starting a new approach to work, to ensure we don't lose the lessons from the mistakes of the past.

WE SUPPORT EACH OTHER FULLY & TREAT LOYAL PEOPLE LIKE FAMILY

This is a community where we look out for our neighbours

Value Description

At Presta Materials, we pride ourselves on being community-minded. We support each other fully and treat each other like a caring, encouraging family. This extends beyond the walls of the organisation. We treat customers, suppliers and even competitors who treat us with loyalty, respect and integrity the same way.

We strongly believe that this attitude is what sets us apart. Our people are our greatest asset, and we invest heavily in their development and well-being. We give each other opportunities to grow professionally and personally, and we support each other through thick and thin. We build relationships with everyone from a starting point of trust and loyalty, and we work hard to maintain this relationship.

In everything we do, we strive to create a company that feels like a community.

Definitive Commitments

- We will always assume good intent in the actions of others until proven otherwise
- We will never cheat or act in any way that breaks the trust in our community
- We will always reach out to people I think need help and support them
- We will actively build relationships as part of our daily work
- We will never be too busy if one of our community is in need

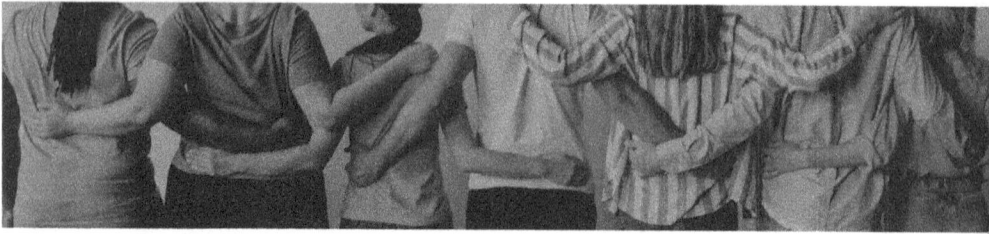

We support each other fully & treat loyal people like family

Essential Story

When Ben's son was diagnosed with cancer, everyone rallied around for support. Jenny worked with the Leadership Team to move all of Ben's tasks to other people so he could spend time at home for an extended period of time. She also organised for video equipment to arrive at his house so he could film handover notes from home rather than come into the office or sit on video calls.

Rick appealed to the Board to sign off a special payment to help the family with expenses. Vanessa organised a fundraiser with some of our closest suppliers and customers. The event was able to raise $250,000 which Ben insisted be donated to the local children's hospital. Jenny, Rick and Vanessa instigated all of this within 5 days of Ben's announcement about his son.

Ben's son is now in remission and regularly joins his father on family days in the office. Ben and Vanessa also run a fundraiser for the hospital which is one of our biggest events each year for our loyal customers and suppliers.

Key Processes - ways we have embedded the guiding principles into our routine

- **Connection Quarterly -** Each quarter, the entire team books out a local restaurant and everyone is invited to attend. Not only does this include staff, but also their families. There is no set agenda and games are conducted throughout the evening to encourage people to spend time with everyone in our broader community.

- **Flex to Complete Policy -** When deadlines will impact our health or the quality of our work, everyone has the discretion to initiate a discussion to review the scope and timelines. If a Flex to Complete conversation is dismissed, this should be immediately escalated to a senior leader.

- **Volunteer Leave & Pooling -** Every employee is able to take 3 days per year to volunteer for a community-building cause. Any employee can also gift their allocation volunteer days to any other member of the team. All volunteering is recorded and captured and we have an annual award for the most community-minded volunteer called the Benny Award.

GUIDING PRINCIPLE 4

WE WANT TO MAKE A POSITIVE IMPACT ON THE WORLD.

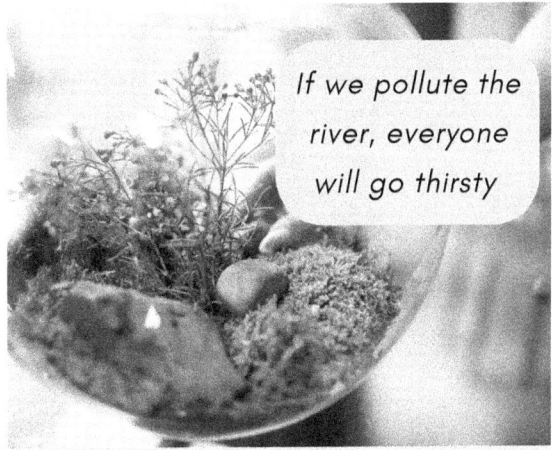

If we pollute the river, everyone will go thirsty

Value Description

As a manufacturing company, we have always been aware of the impact our processes, equipment and products have on the environment and the communities we live and work. Now more than ever, we are committed to minimising our environmental footprint and helping our customers and competitors to do the same.

We are always considering the impact of our decisions on the broader community. We are focused on developing products with a reduced environmental impact, as well as manufacturing processes that are less resource-intensive. In addition, we will be working with our suppliers and customers to help them reduce their environmental impact and increase the positive impact they have on the community. Our ultimate goal is to build sustainable, healthy communities that have a positive impact on the world for generations to come.

Definitive Commitments

- We will never make a business decision that intentionally harms our communities
- We will always conduct environmental risk assessments for projects
- We will not work with suppliers or customers who damage the community
- We will actively seek ways to reduce our negative impact and increase social cohesion

We want to make a positive impact on the world.

Essential Story

Francis noticed that one of our major suppliers, APK, was sending us a lot of products wrapped in unnecessary amounts of non-recyclable plastic. One day, Francis read an article about a local company, GoodWrap, manufacturing a biodegradable alternative for packaging. She reached out to the APK and asked if she could find an alternative that matched their current costs, would they change to an alternative packaging.

They agreed, so Francis gathered some of their costs and asked GoodWrap for a proposal to supply the alternative packaging. While their solution was more expensive, Vanessa calculated the reduced costs for our own waste disposal would more than offset the difference.

Working with the Leadership Team, Presta Materials was able to sign a contract with GoodWrap and APK that reduces Presta's landfill waste and haulage, reduces APK's packaging costs and creates new jobs in our local community. GoodWrap has also become a Presta customer and is a regular contributor to our annual fundraiser.

Key Processes - ways we have embedded the guiding principles into our routines

- **Waste Reduction Target -** At Presta, we have the goal of reducing our non-recyclable and non-reusable waste each year. Every year this target is achieved, every employee at Presta Materials receives a financial bonus.

- **Skilled Mentoring Program -** All skilled technicians with more than 5 years of service at Presta are encouraged to enter a mentoring program at the local TAFE. This enables our most skilled workers to share their knowledge and experience with new apprentices in our community. They don't need to join Presta at the end, wherever they go we hope they take a little of the Presta magic with them.

- **Volunteer Leave & Pooling -** Every employee is able to take 3 days per year to volunteer for a community-building cause. Any employee can also gift their allocation volunteer days to any other member of the team. All volunteering is recorded and captured and we have an annual award for the most community-minded volunteer called the Benny Award.

WE EMBRACE CHALLENGING QUESTIONS AND PUSH EACH OTHER TO IMPROVE.

You don't train hard to make it easier, you train hard to go faster

Value Description

At Presta Materials, we never shy away from a challenge. The world around us is changing at an incredible pace and the manufacturing sector is no different. Our competitors are always evolving and improving, and we need to be constantly pushing ourselves to stay ahead of the curve. Embracing challenging questions and different opinions is essential to our success. It helps us to identify areas where we need to improve and inspires us to try harder next time. This culture of constant challenge is what drives us. It's how we always strive to be better than we were yesterday, and how we continue to innovate and grow.

We encourage everyone to ask questions and challenge each other at all levels. We believe that this is the best way for us all to learn and grow. We want everyone to know that you have the authority to ask questions and challenge the ideas of anyone.

Definitive Commitments

- We will never dismiss someone who questions us or challenges our ideas
- We will always ask questions to clarify or challenge ideas we don't agree with
- We will actively seek out the opinions of people who might disagree with us
- We will always encourage others to ask questions and challenge us
- We will actively disagree without being disagreeable to our peers

We embrace challenging questions and push each other to improve.

Essential Story

A new project had been given the green light by the Leadership Team. Vanessa took the proposal to her Sales and asked them to give their opinions. After a few minutes of thoughtful consideration, Ivan challenged a number of the underlying assumptions in the business case. "Wait a second," he said skeptically. "I'm not sure that this is going to work. These numbers feel way too high for this part of the economic cycle."

Vanessa was initially taken aback. She'd been so excited about the new project idea. But after doing some additional research, they found that there was actually an error in the original calculations. If they went ahead with the project based on those numbers, it would have cost Presta hundreds of thousands of dollars.

Ivan and Vanessa worked together to develop the Red Team Gate to ensure all projects are rigorously challenged. Ivan was also asked to support the project team in rescoping the project. He was given the first-ever Fix It Award at Presta Materials.

Key Processes - ways we have embedded the guiding principles into our routine

- **Red Team Gate -** Every project or proposal at Presta must pass a Red Team Gate. This is where a team of people is selected to actively challenge and find flaws in a new proposal. The team is to simulate worst-case scenarios or sophisticated competitors that can impact projects. The Red Team must sign off before it will proceed.

- **The Fixed It Awards -** Each quarter, 5 people who have found new ways of improving or made an error and fixed it successfully are invited to present a short case study of their situation to the entire organisation at a celebration event. We then all vote for the best example and the winner is issued with a Fixed It trophy and prize.

- **Written before Spoken** - When capturing ideas from a team on a number of options, the person asking must provide all information without providing their opinion on which option. Everyone is then asked to write down their opinions on a piece of paper. We then ask everyone to share what they have read to avoid the natural dangers of extrovert bias, anchoring and group thinking.

WHAT NEXT?

Using the playbook

This playbook is not a rule book or a process manual. Don't expect it will tell you what to do. Instead, it is a guide for all of the decisions (big and small) that you will need to make each day. While we have a lot of processes and rules for the way we manufacture certain things, most of the work you do as a human will rely on you making subjective decisions in ambiguous situations. This is where you can refer to the playbook.

You will also spend time interacting with other people here at Presta. After reading and digesting this playbook, you should have a better understanding of what to expect from them and they will have an idea of what to expect of you. Our behaviours set our culture, so how we do things around here should be in line with the playbook.

If this is your first time reading this, don't freak out. We all know it takes time to understand, remember and implement these guiding principles into your daily work and you will find everyone here will be supportive as you find your groove, it is guiding principle #3 after all.

Feedback is vital

Our machines have dials, sensors and warning systems to tell us when things are not working properly or causing an issue. This is vital in manufacturing. Unfortunately, humans don't have dials and sometimes when we are causing issues, we don't notice ourselves. This is why feedback is vital.

You are encouraged to give feedback at any time you think necessary, there is never a bad time. As you will find, if you give feedback in alignment with our guiding principles, people will be more likely to receive it with the kindness it is given.

You will receive feedback. It is important for everyone to receive feedback as an opportunity to grow. There may be times you feel the feedback was not appropriate, it can always happen in a messy world. You are invited to resolve it supportively with the person directly, discuss it with others in the organisation to resolve it effectively or go to a member of the Leadership Team for support. You are never alone.

PRESTA
MATERIALS

Get engaged in the community

Community and culture are our competitive advantages. We encourage all employees to get involved in the community and contribute to the culture. Have coffee with your team, chat with your manager, and go for lunch with someone in another team. The more we get to understand each other, the better we are, so don't wait, be active.

In fact, if this is your first read of this document, we recommend the next step is a conversation with people in your team. Coffee is on us!

What if these guiding principles don't work?

There may be times when you feel the guiding principles aren't a good fit or that you need to break one of our guiding principles to do your job. Here is what to do:

Step 1: Don't break them, yet.

The guiding principles are very important to us. Breaking them is a very serious thing to do, so as a first step if you feel you should maybe look for another option. Consult with some other people and see what they think. There are many ways to do everything and we are all here to help.

Step 2: Challenge our Leadership Team first

The guiding principles are great but we don't expect they will never change. If you feel something is not right, speak with one of our leadership team about it first. Suggest changes and have discussions around how we can make them better. The leadership team wants this to be a great place to work so we always want to hear from you.

Step 3: Maybe it's just not for you

If after discussions with the leadership team you are still at a point where you feel the guiding principles are not right, this might not be the right place. No company is perfect for everyone and the last thing we want is for you to feel working here compromises your values. If you find yourself in this position, speak with your people leader. We will support you in making a positive transition into a place where you can live your values and not feel tension with our guiding principles. No hard feelings, we just want the best for you and our entire Presta community.

PRESTA
MATERIALS

About Empathic Consulting

WHY WE EXIST

At Empathic Consulting, we believe understanding people is critical for us to build a better world. This means empathy is the most important capability to create improved outcomes for businesses, leaders and communities. While too often ignored or misunderstood, empathy is the capacity for a person to understand the rational and emotional drivers of others. When leaders and businesses can develop this skill to build and understanding of their employees, customers and stakeholders, they are able to develop breakthrough competitive strategies and foster powerful teams through greater diversity and employee engagement.

OUR PURPOSE

Empathic Consulting exists to create a world with more understanding, compassion and connection powered by empathic leaders.

Join us in our mission to change the world!

- ✉ daniel@empathicconsulting.com
- 🌐 www.empathicconsulting.com
- (in) www.linkedin.com/in/daniel-empathicconsulting/
- ▶ www.youtube.com/channel/UCyeDz8NFz-Z69-LZBoBlm1Q/featured

WHAT CLIENTS SAY

" *Thought inspiring, provoking and interesting. Took you through the the emotional journey of using empathy in your business.*

Robbie Cooke, CEO, Tyro Payments

" *Fantastic both in content and delivery. I was looking for someone to open up other ways of approaching leadership and looking at our business environment and they delivered!*

Michaela Flanagan, Head of Branch Operations, Swiss Re

" *I can honestly say it was one of the best sessions I have been a part of. The content was unique & very interactive. I highly recommend Empathic Consulting to build empathy & understanding to drive performance.*

Daniel Markovski, Group Sales Manager, Nova

" *They engaged people who I didn't think would ever respond, let alone take-away actions. Post this session, I observed genuine behaviour changes. This was one of the best things I have done for the team.*

Rochelle Eldridge, Executive Manager, CBA

Printed book ISBN 978 0 6453665 0 1

Publisher: The Book Adviser
BN 61 747 410 514
Website: www.thebookadviser.com.au

Cover and internal design: Rasika UM, www.shashika.info
Proofreader: Clare Wadsworth

Aligning Culture & Strategy

www.ingramcontent.com/pod-product-compliance
Lightning Source LLC
Chambersburg PA
CBHW071426210326
41597CB00020B/3663